HOW TO
GROW
YOUR DENTAL PRACTICE
IN THE NEW ECONOMY

HOW TO

GROW

YOUR DENTAL PRACTICE

IN THE NEW ECONOMY

KEY STRATEGIES TO

PREDICTABLE, SIGNIFICANT

AND **SUSTAINABLE** RESULTS

JOHN COTTON

Advantage®

Published by Advantage, Charleston, South Carolina.
Member of Advantage Media Group.

ADVANTAGE is a registered trademark and the Advantage colophon is a trademark of Advantage Media Group, Inc.

Printed in the United States of America.

ISBN: 978-1-59932-485-2
LCCN: 2014938957

Book design by Megan Elger.

This publication is designed to provide accurate and authoritative information in regard to the subject matter covered. It is sold with the understanding that the publisher is not engaged in rendering legal, accounting, or other professional services. If legal advice or other expert assistance is required, the services of a competent professional person should be sought.

 Advantage Media Group is proud to be a part of the Tree Neutral® program. Tree Neutral offsets the number of trees consumed in the production and printing of this book by taking proactive steps such as planting trees in direct proportion to the number of trees used to print books. To learn more about Tree Neutral, please visit www.treeneutral.com. To learn more about Advantage's commitment to being a responsible steward of the environment, please visit www.advantagefamily.com/green

Advantage Media Group is a publisher of business, self-improvement, and professional development books and online learning. We help entrepreneurs, business leaders, and professionals share their Stories, Passion, and Knowledge to help others Learn & Grow. Do you have a manuscript or book idea that you would like us to consider for publishing? Please visit advantagefamily.com or call 1.866.775.1696.

TABLE OF CONTENTS

ACKNOWLEDGMENTS

My thanks to Lisa McDaniel, Senior Vice President of Dental Team Performance, and our holding company, BestBIZ, LLC. She is the epitome of a true partner. Lisa's knowledge, experience, expertise, and unwavering work ethic are a big part of clients' successes. She has withstood my relentless barrage of new ideas, strategies, and test projects to better serve our clients' needs. Lisa is a unique talent, taking a framework idea and converting it to a results-based strategy. Her talents and skills, supported by her character and integrity, are foundational to our mission of doing the right thing for our clients and their team members. For these reasons, and many more, I am forever grateful for Lisa McDaniel.

Kevin J. Alexander, DMD, my neighbor, friend, and dentist—call it luck, happenstance, or the grace of God, but when Kevin asked me a few business questions on a Saturday morning in October 2008, neither of us could have possibly expected the outcome. One year later, Kevin's practice would have a record year at the height of the recession. And his practice would post record years each year after that, fueled by a committed team. Dental Team Performance would become another division of our company and we would serve over 350 dentists in 34 states and three countries. Kevin, I'm so glad you had a few questions! Because of you, our eyes have been opened to the exciting world of dentists and dental practices. Thank you for your friendship, your trust, and your confidence.

Of course, this book wouldn't exist without the early adopter dentists who saw that something we were doing made sense for them and their practices. We appreciate your trust and faith in us. And we thank the hundreds of other dentists who followed by honoring us with the pleasure to serve them. To the team members representing these dentists, thank you for the opportunity to be a part of your lives by serving you.

Dentists know the challenges of being a producer, while running a business. For that matter, the majority of business owners know the same challenges. I'm in the same camp with you, and have been for over 27 years. I've launched, built, merged, and transitioned a combination of six businesses in several industries. As I look back, the first few were built on prayers, luck, and a big dose of persistence. I knew what to do for our clients, but the operational side of running a business wasn't taught in college, even to someone like me, with a major in business administration. Courses in marketing, personnel management, accounting, expense management, communications, and strategic planning offered me textbook knowledge, but not the practical application of the knowledge. Unfortunately, for us business owners, on-the-job training is required training, making mistakes is part of the process, and continuously learning from innovative thinkers helps us know what to do and what *not* to do.

Based on my personal experiences of running my own businesses and serving more than 1,200 client businesses, it is clear that the business leaders, big and small, who achieve the highest levels of revenue and profit find internal and/or external professionals to optimize the operational health of their organizations. Dental Team Performance is an organization that choses to cover the basics of operations internally and outsource what we can't do or don't want to do internally. Every industry is supported by a long list of specialists serving a wide variety of areas, from operational efficiencies and effectiveness to marketing to human resources and more. The business of private practice dentistry, as you know, is similarly stocked with the right professional at the right time for the right need. Name a Fortune 500 company and you'll find multiple outsourced specialists engaged at any given time. None of us know everything we need to know to be as successful as we can be. I can pretend to know everything and neglect obvious needs, and in both cases, I'll suffer the consequences of lower revenue, ineffective team performance, lower net profit, and a plethora of other frustrations that are preventable. I can find those who can help me achieve my goals and reap the rewards sooner. That reminds me of a dentist who engaged our firm a few years ago and I've never forgotten her comment to me as we wrapped up our last meeting. She said, "Don't tell any other dentist what we are doing because they will think something is wrong with my practice." I was blown away by her way of thinking. We helped her improve production by 19 percent in six months and her team was, for the first time ever, committed, performing at a high level, and very happy. No business is ever perfect! We business owners have to realize that the goal isn't perfection; it's optimization.

The best-of-the-best companies on the planet seek assistance from trusted advisers to optimize strategic and tactical improvements, because the skill sets and expertise don't exist internally. A dental practice is no different. The do-it-yourselfers often pay a steep price because their expected results don't occur, production suffers, team members push back, and time and effort are wasted. Further, in trying to save money on professional advice, the actual net return on time, people, and investment is negative, not positive. I don't do plumbing and electrical work. I call the professionals. I suppose I could have installed the invisible fence for my dog, but I didn't. I can brush my teeth and floss as you prefer, but I can't repair the crack in #3. Why would dentists/business owners deny themselves bigger and faster success by attempting to do something in their practice in which they are not the most proficient? I'm working with a business coach on a very big project at this writing. The project includes a legal document. Am I going to write my own agreement? No! An attorney specializing in my specific need has been engaged. Also, I elected to engage a copywriter to help with a big part of the marketing strategy. That's three consultants for one project. I wrote the content for this book without a consultant, but publishing it requires a publisher. Smart people seek professional expertise. They decide, act, and move forward by engaging people who can get results faster, more effectively, and more efficiently.

As a dentist, you know about the trials and tribulations of producing great work all day, and then trying to handle the operational side of your practice in your spare time. There are times when everything seems to click, and there are plenty of times when the frustration is overwhelming. A hygienist quits and now you have to find a replacement. Collections seem low, but why? When you left the office yesterday afternoon, the schedule was full. This morning you have too many holes in the hygiene schedule and your one decent operatory case for the day just cancelled. All hands on deck for recall and chart audits to find warm bodies to fill these holes. Oops! Payroll is due today. Are you overstaffed or underperforming? You know you need to consider going chartless, but is it really a priority? You know an intraoral camera is a good investment, but will it really make a difference? What if your team members don't use it? Should you upgrade your software or wait? Your dental assistant just called in sick. The practice down the street is very much like yours, but you heard they are doing $300,000 more per year than you. What are they doing that you aren't?

"IF I COULD JUST DO DENTISTRY."

The Degree of Success on the Operational Side of a Dental Practice Dictates the Degree of Success in Production, Collections, and Profit

The purpose of this book is to help you create more production, collections, and profit in a manner that best serves your patients, your team members, and you, the dentist/owner. While we are at it, why not reduce the stress and frustration of running your practice, so that you and your team can do more dentistry and reduce the worry about the day-to-day operations?

In dental school you probably received a sampling of practice management resources, but very little information on the practical application and details of strategic planning and the execution of your plan. You probably did not learn how to hire the best team members, how set expectations, how to lead your team to achieve your expectations, and so on and so on and so on. Continuing-education lectures for practice management traditionally offer very good information, but it comes in small pieces without integration into your practice, your team, your market, and your patient mix. And nothing prepares you and your team for the cause and effect of the ever-changing economy, patient behaviors, and competition for patients. Filling the schedule is a must, but too many no-shows and cancellations and too few new patients and referrals are costly. And what about all of those patients who do not accept, schedule, and complete treatment? That's a big one where production vanishes into never-never land.

Whether you are new in private practice, you have decades of experience, or are considering selling your practice, the effectiveness of your business operations matters, and it matters a lot. It's your economic engine. Think of your practice as a train track. One rail is clinical and the other rail is operational. The train can't be effective without parallel rails. This is true for any private practice, whether it is that of an MD, attorney, plumber, or electrician. The operational side of your practice/business has to deliver the maximum opportunities in order for you and your team to deliver the maximum amount of dentistry your patients want and need.

How to Grow Your Dental Practice in the New Economy is based on the actual results achieved in 343 dental practices in 34 U.S. states, Canada, and Australia during the *bad* economy. It isn't about theories, ideas, or concepts. It is about how to achieve predictable, significant, and sustainable results.

Foundationally, it is imperative that any strategy or tactic you wish to undertake be designed to create a winning outcome for patients, team members, and you. If not, it will live a short life and you will be back to square one. I know, because I personally learned this expensive lesson several times.

> *Foundationally, it is imperative that any strategy or tactic you wish to undertake be designed to create a winning outcome for patients, team members, and you. If not, it will live a short life and you will be back to square one. I know, because I personally learned this expensive lesson several times.*

To help this book help you, a little background might be useful. I quit counting a long time ago, but let's just say we have served more than 1,200 business owners in multiple industries, with 33,000-plus team members in 44 states. Collectively, these clients have added more than $400,000,000 of sustainable revenue. While each industry and business has unique characteristics and special needs, there is one absolute common denominator: the people. That means customers and patients, team members, and owners. People do business with people, not with businesses. People serve other people's needs. People work for people. People hire people. In Chapter One, we'll make sure this foundational topic is illuminated.

Our introduction to the dental industry was not planned. From 1999 to 2007 we served more than 350 community bank clients in 31 states and were endorsed by eight state bank associations. Based on our services, our bank clients were enjoying a very healthy return on investment. Life was good! In our 2007 year-end strategic planning, we decided, for long-term growth, it would be wise to diversify the industries we served. So, we invested a little time, effort, and money to do so. Be it inspiration, common sense, or the grace of God, the diversification of our client base was timely. The entire banking industry, especially community banks, was beginning to experience the devastation of the crumbling mortgage industry, which devastated the U.S. economy and many of our clients. They were not too big to fail, so hundreds of them did. Needless to say, we were affected. Of course, you have been affected by the Great Recession too. Now what? Fight or flight?

My team and I battened down the hatches and accelerated our business development to diversify our client mix. Then, on a fateful Saturday morning in 2008, I was headed to my outside basement door while my next-door neighbor (and good friend) Kevin was coming around the corner of his house. We exchanged greetings and laughed about our "honey do" list. Then, he asked a few business questions. Since Kevin Alexander is my dentist, I knew his team but not so much about his business. With our dogs barking, we decided to meet for lunch the following week to discuss his interests and concerns. Little did I know the dental industry was about to become a big part of my business life.

Interestingly, the questions and overarching concerns of that initial lunch meeting with Kevin have been repeated over and over by hundreds of other dentists across the USA. As a result of that meeting, my team and I helped Kevin and his team, beginning with the creation of a strategic plan tailored to his specific needs, his team members, and his patient mix. Then, we helped him execute his plan. By the end of 2009, in the middle of the recession, Kevin's practice had increased production by $105,432 over his 2008 numbers, a record year for him. He was ecstatic! Since then, his production has continued to increase with year-over-year records and a five-year overall increase in collections of 42 percent. Yes, he's an advocate of Dental Team Performance—and a raving fan. He referred us to his study group and then to the Birmingham District Dental Society and was instrumental in our endorsement by the Alabama Dental Association as well as a host of other important relationships. Within three years, dentists in 34 states would be served by DTP.

Thank you, Kevin!

Based on our prior depth and breadth of business experiences and proven results with multiple industries, we already owned a toolbox of comprehensive best-of-the-best performance

strategies and tactics to achieve success for our clients. So, how can a strategy, tactic, or concept from a community bank, a commercial pipefitter, or a tech company apply to a dental practice? Easy! The operational health of any business is about the *people*: the team members, the customers, and the leadership. It is not so much about what the business delivers. Your team members dictate your production. What they do, how they do it, when they do it, where they do it and the results they achieve are as important to the success of your practice as the dentistry.

This book will, I hope, open your mind to more creative, strategic, and realistic thinking and help you focus on the most important factors that matter most to your practice. I'll offer proven methods to help you create a team of self-motivated performers, and to enhance the desire of your patients to want to do business with your practice. I call them the innovative fundamentals. Innovation is all around us. Remember when your front desk team had to confirm every appointment with a telephone call. Now you can cut call time in half and achieve better results with Revenue Well, Demand Force, and a host of other such services. How about intraoral cameras and CAD/CAM technology? Going chartless? Innovation is here. What about your strategies, tactics, and protocols that improve team performance to fill the schedule and optimize completed treatment plans? Where is the innovation? That's the million-dollar question!

What about fundamentals? Take the core principle of people doing business with people in a very personal business such as a dental practice. Doesn't it make sense to find the most professional methods of helping patients to *want* to do business with your practice? Solutions are plentiful, but which solution is best for you and your practice? Trial and error is not a good way to find the best solution, since team members despise being guinea pigs. A solution isn't about trying more new ideas or working harder. It's about defining a performance-based solution that fits your practice and your team with the accompanying specific protocol that achieves your desired results. You want more new patients. You want your active patients to show up for prophylaxis (prophy) and not cancel or become no-shows. You want your patients to accept, schedule, and complete your diagnosed treatment. And, yes, you want your patients to refer their friends to you. The right solution is what you want.

My hope for you is that you open your mind to the *innovative fundamentals* that will allow you to achieve a team of performers, less stress, and an entirely new level of production and collections. It's in you and in your team members. If you are a sports fan, you know about the fundamentals. For example, I can step onto the first tee of a golf course with the best equipment available, but if I do not use the fundamentals of a very good golf swing, it's going to be a miserable round of golf —not successful by any measurement. Football? Fundamentals are everywhere, from blocking and tackling to pass patterns and the proper quarterback handoff to the running back. The fundamentals must be in place or the results will be ugly. Pick your sport and you will see that fundamentals are critical. Pick the most successful businesses, including many dental practices, and you will see that the fundamentals are well thought out, aligned, and expected to happen consistently.

How about your practice? Are your fundamentals in place? Are you sure? How about innovation? In college football, the spread offense with a quarterback threat dominates the game. What about you and your practice? What's your innovation? What is that unique value proposition that differentiates your practice from the others? Patients vote to appoint or not. They vote to show up or not. They vote to complete treatment or not. What are your *innovative funda-*

mentals that move prospective patients and your active patients to vote for you and your practice? You have it, but have you unleashed it? That's where you want to be. That's where you can be. And, it's your choice.

But I can hear it now. "Sure, John, you can hype all of this wishful thinking, but you aren't dealing with the bad economy, or with patients who are no-shows, or cancel, or can't afford the treatment they need and don't pay their bills when we provide treatment." Actually, my team and I are involved with hundreds of practices of all shapes and sizes, in small towns and big cities, from GP family practices taking every insurance contract to high-end, fee-for-service cosmetic practices to combination pediatric and ortho groups. There are very few key differences between practices that are thriving and those that are just surviving. The thriving practices are led by people who do not accept mediocrity and are relentlessly committed to finding their focus and staying focused on the few critical strategies that affect patients' votes in favor of their practices. They have simplified their practice operations and focused on the few areas that have the biggest impact on results.

It's Not about Working Harder or Smarter; It's about Performing Better with Focus

The contents of this book are meant to challenge you, your way of thinking, and your actions. But, there is no cookie-cutter quick-fix and no pixie dust or magic wand.

Several years ago, I was meeting with a community bank president in western North Carolina. He and a few key employees had formed the bank a few years earlier and had grown it from a storefront in a strip mall to one of the fastest growing community banks in the country. The bank president had engaged our company to help with team performance strategies and tactics. I asked him to define the unique value the bank provides for its customers. Without pause, he said, "John, our banking products and services are no different from other banks', but we deliver such a high level of consistently exceptional experiences for our customers that word-of-mouth referrals have built this bank from one branch to twelve." Two years later, a big bank offered the stockholders a buy-out deal that they couldn't refuse. Cha-Ching! Dentistry is your product. What's your unique value? What drives people to want to come to you and your practice? What drives them to want to refer their friends, relatives, and neighbors? The answers lie in you, your focus, and your leadership's commitment to a value proposition your patients see, feel, and experience.

Make notes in the margins of this book, underline key messages, and tag your favorite pages. More importantly, open your mind to the possibility of finding your laser-like focus in the few key strategies that matter most to the success of your practice. Bolster your fundamentals and find your innovation. When you do that, you will be able to find predictable, significant, and sustainable results.

CHAPTER ONE

BREAK THE REAR VIEW MIRROR: SEE YOUR FUTURE

STRATEGY #1

I remember when my dad arrived to pick me up from Pop Warner football practice when I was a kid. It was 1965 and he arrived in a brand-new Ford Galaxy. It had electric windows, air conditioning, and a three-speed automatic transmission. Today my five-year-old car has GPS, a traffic indicator, a weather alert system, heated seats, a six-speed automatic transmission, and run-flat tires. When I went to college in 1970, my mother bought me a calculator that could add, subtract, multiply, and divide, and it cost $100. Today the same calculator functions can be purchased for less than $5 (I just bought one at Walgreen's). Change happens. In the mid-1970s the business world was, to a large extent, industrial. The Internet didn't exist.

Today, technology affects all of us. Improvements happen. The rear view picture is the past. Try driving your car by looking in the rear view mirror—actually, don't do that! If you want to arrive at your destination, looking through the front windshield is probably a good idea. Try running your dental practice successfully by operating it as you did 20, 15, 10, or even 5 years ago. If you do, your practice will suffer. We all know of practices that have withered to an unnecessary end. That's a shame, because it doesn't have to be that way. Does this mean you should make radical changes? Not at all! In fact, small but strategic improvements often provide the biggest benefits. The main thing is to think strategically and act tactically. Which small improvement matters most? In other words, invest in thought and preparation on the front end. Once you are clear on the strategy, you can think about and develop the tactics that will make the strategy successful, as the dentist did who called me a few days ago. He is a solo GP dentist in a middle-class market, collecting just over $1.5 million, with three full-time hygienists. By most measurements, he is doing quite well, but he wanted to know what he could do to make sure that he and his team members were focused on the right things and were not overlooking something that mattered. I congratulated him on his success, and he said that he and his team were continuously looking for ways to improve. This is the kind of mindset that optimizes production and collections. At this writing, we have finished developing his strategic plan and he is on the path to his improvements.

STRATEGY #1: THE PATIENT EXPERIENCE

In the dental practice world, innovative business improvements are all around, including digital X-rays, digital files, intraoral cameras, CAD/CAM technology, lasers, office and operatory design, patient contact software, and much more. All of these improvements can improve efficiency for the practice and perhaps provide a better dental experience for patients. Great! But your patients experience similar innovations in many of the other businesses that they encounter in their daily life. We are bombarded every day with more than 3,000 marketing messages attempting to extract our hard-earned money from our hands. The competition for your patient's wallet is ever increasing.

Your biggest competitor is your patient's mindset. Consumers' mindsets are affected by the hundreds of other businesses, including online organizations that incessantly pander for a share of consumers' money. Think about how Apple, Zappos, BestBuy, Home Depot, automobile dealers, grocery stores, and hundreds of other customer-savvy businesses communicate with us to gain market and wallet share.

> *Your biggest competitor is your patient's mindset.*

You might say, "But I don't have their marketing budget." Forget the budget. *How* do they communicate with us? The answer is that their messages are jammed with the emotional benefits of their products and services, and their brand image. The mantra of Publix grocery stores is "Where it's a pleasure to shop." This short tagline says nothing about food. It's all about emotion–in this case, pleasure. At Home Depot, a concierge employee greets you when you enter to help direct you to what you need. Zappos makes it easy to shop online, with short product videos to entice you. And you can buy and return items for free until you are completely satisfied. Apple stores? Well, you just have to experience them to understand the value they create. Their customers often become advocates of Apple to the nth degree. Oh, by the way, an Apple store is a perfect example of how an organization can create an environment where the customer graduates from a *need* to a *want*. Look around and you'll see a cross-section of every economic and social class buying high-end electronics. Think about that previous sentence in the context of a dental practice: graduating from a *need* to a *want*.

Granted, some businesses are designed for low cost and that's their brand, but that's not your brand. If your value proposition is focused on price, you'll need to work 12 hours per day six days per week to make a decent living. If consumers were as price conscious as many dentists and team members believe, we would all drive the cheapest car, live in the cheapest home, and eat hot dogs and PB&J sandwiches. But our actions demonstrate otherwise and tell us that the vast majority of consumers want value. *Value?* What's value? The product or service has to fit our needs, that's a given. But how we feel about the product or service matters just as much. Furthermore, how we feel about the experience we have with the people offering the product or service has just as much to do with our decisions as the product itself. I can cash checks, deposit checks, and do my banking online at any bank. So, why do I do business with ServisFirst Bank? Look at their name. They practice what they preach.

My son and his wife just purchased a new car. They had a price range in mind. They analyzed cars based on looks, driveability, gas mileage, and accessories. They narrowed their choices down to three and bought the most expensive of the three because they "just liked it better and the people at the dealership were very helpful and not pushy." Bingo! The value for the winning dealership was its helpfulness without pushiness. It's all about how we *feel*. All things being reasonably equal, how we feel (emotion) is the value we consumers seek. Logically, we'll state a different reason for a purchase, but the reality states otherwise. For a dental practice, it's the same story, the same answer. How we feel dictates the value. If the price is reasonable, your patients will make decisions that affect your production based on how they feel about your practice, which means you, your team, and every other indicator that affects feelings.

How we feel about a business is also measured by our experiences with other businesses. More precisely, it's about the *people* in those other businesses. Call it customer service, if you like. But it's far more than just service. Customer service is old school. It's in the rear view mirror. In today's economy it's about the overall customer experience, the totality of every touch point that can possibly affect how we feel, whether it is on the telephone, in the office, or online. Every communication method (verbal, written, e-mail, and text), and the professional manner in which it is delivered, impacts how we feel about an organization. Ritz-Carlton hotels are well known for their customer experience. But their customers pay for it. Mercedes, BMW, and Lexus can manufacture a great car, but rest assured, if the customer experience isn't consistently exceptional, the customer will go elsewhere. We've all made the decision to not return to a business, and that decision is rarely based on the product. It is most often based on the customer experience we received from someone in the business. It may have been bad or indifferent, and neither of those experiences gives us the urge to return and do business with those people (business) again.

Unless your practice is in Beverly Hills or another ultra-affluent market, the economic status of your regular patients can vary greatly. So, consider the customer experience in businesses that serve basic needs: pharmacies, grocery stores, clothing stores, and even Amazon. com. Just as you are, these businesses are trying to accomplish two primary objectives, 1) they want more customers—market share, and 2) they want to retain their customers for repeat business— wallet share. I don't pretend to be an expert in marketing, but a casual observer knows that these businesses offer products that their customers want. They appeal to their customer niche by offering buy-one-get-one-free specials, coupons, rewards programs, and referral programs. They focus on packaging, presentation, product placement, and customer flow. They connect with their customers frequently via e-mail, text, and direct mail. They advertise their brand to keep their name in front of would-be customers. Blocking and tackling—the fundamentals! All of this is very important, but the biggest *value* proposition is creating and maintaining the highest level of the customer experience.

I was a keynote speaker for a study club a few weeks ago and part of my presentation was about the patient experience. After my presentation, several dentists came up to me. One of the dentists said, "John, I've been practicing dentistry for 38 years. Not many years ago, all I had to do was show up at my practice and do dentistry all day. Life was very good! Now, I can't assume anything. I have to reinvent the way I think. Thank you!"

While there are plenty of businesses engaging in customer acquisition and retention programs, the most successful ones stand out and differentiate themselves. The leaders of these categories, defined by profitability, know how to create an environment that delivers the best experiences for their customers. They know that emotion (how we feel) is a key driver of buying decisions. Therefore, these businesses intentionally optimize top-line and bottom-line results by converting more "tire kickers" to paying customers. They know that customers are far more apt to return and buy again and again if they continue to feel good about their experiences. That could be considered innovative, but, surely, it's fundamental!

Look at Southwest Airlines. That company has the ugliest planes in the sky and no first-class seating. It rarely offers the lowest cost for flights, but it is more profitable than any other airline and has been for 20-plus years. Every other airline in business today has filed for bankruptcy at least once. So what's driving SWA's profitability? The customer experience! A very large number of people *want* to fly with an airline that demonstrates that it cares about its customers. Even the SWA website is customer-centric. And get this: The first birthday card I receive every year comes from SWA. That company gets it!

You might say, "But John, our team members are very nice and friendly!" With all due respect, there is a big difference between being nice and friendly and delivering consistently exceptional customer experiences. Just ask your patients. That big difference translates into fewer no-shows, fewer cancellations, more referrals, more new patients, more completed treatment plans, and lower accounts receivable. The end result is *big* improvements in your production and collections. You be the judge. Take a look at the chart below.

THE RESULTS OF OPTIMIZING THE PATIENT EXPERIENCE

✓	No-shows:	2 fewer per week
✓	Cancellations:	2 fewer per week
✓	New patients:	1 more per week
✓	Referrals:	1 more per week
✓	Recare/recall:	2 more per week
	Total per week:	8 more patients seen per week
	Total per month:	32 more patients seen per month
	Total results:	$10,000+/- in new production per month

How do you react to a business where a team member, manager, or the owner consistently makes you feel he or she really cares about you and appreciates you? Most of us react with a tendency to do something nice for those who do something nice for us. It's called the law of reciprocity: we reciprocate. So, when we need a product or service that the business offers, we buy from it and the price is rarely an issue. Conversely, when you are treated as a number and feel you are not appreciated, or the overall attitude toward you is one of indifference, what do you do? Many customers/patients quietly take their business elsewhere. Their feet and credit card move on and they don't look back. That's reciprocation too, but in the wrong direction.

It's hard enough to fill the schedule and keep it full. Why not optimize your practice's ability to retain your active patients and improve their interests and willingness to refer their friends? You can!

It's the same story in many dental practices every day. For some patients, cost can be the determining factor, but don't jump to a conclusion. The cost factor can easily be an excuse. The real reason why patients do not appoint and accept treatment is because, more often than not, they don't see, feel, or experience the value compared to the investment. And the value is rarely defined as the dentistry. It's usually the benefits of the dentistry, the patient's motivators, and their overall experience when dealing with your practice. The value can be that your patients' teeth are healthy, their smile is better, crowns beat root canals, the patients trust your diagnosis, they trust the hygienists, they trust the treatment coordinator, they like everyone in the practice, and so on. People do business with people they know, like, and trust. They ramp up their level of all three of these as the emotional connection with you and your team ramps up, which decreases costs as a factor, proportionately.

No doubt, some patients just can't justify the cost of a treatment. That's not your fault and there isn't much you or your team members can do about it. But I'll say it again. Showing up for a prophy appointment or an operatory treatment and paying for it is more about how your patients perceive the value that you and your team members deliver and not so much about the cost. If we want something badly enough, we'll find a way to pay for it! The patient experience *is* the value proposition. It's a basic fundamental of any business, especially in a personal and professional service organization such as a private dental practice. Unlike Ritz-Carlton, where the customer experience is justified by the cost, there is a long list of companies, big and small, international and hometown, that consistently deliver exceptional customer experiences without a price tag that justifies the experience. I already noted Southwest Airlines and Publix supermarkets. Trader Joes, Chick fil-A and Enterprise Rental Cars are well known for their customer experience. But what about a dental practice? Here's a short list of practices that consistently deliver exceptional experiences for their patients:

- Kevin J. Alexander, DMD
- Adreinne Ammons, DDS
- Andalusia Dental Group
- Allen Blackmon, DMD
- Lynsey Brown, DMD
- David Currie, DMD
- Zack Dollar, DMD
- Eufaula Family Dentistry
- Amy Hartsfield, DMD
- Bill Ingram, DMD
- Steve Murpree, DMD
- Reid Roberts, DMD
- Steineker & Dillon, PC
- Eric Swinson, DMD
- René Talbot, DDS
- The Smile Center

- Tucker Family Dentistry, PC
- Rick Verdin, DDS

The before-and-after increase in the production of these practices mirrors the increase in their patient experience measurement scores.

The new economy, post-Great Recession, has forced innovation in a variety of products for virtually every industry. You are well aware of the new and improved products in the dental industry. But patients assume you have to keep up with the times. They want *value*. The overarching value comes down to one of the simplest human needs: feelings. It's about how we feel!

ACTION: THE PATIENT EXPERIENCE

Create an environment in your practice that enhances how your patients feel about you and your team. Perfection is impossible, but being consistently exceptional is expected. Your patients will reward you again and again.

The Patient Experience: How to Optimize It

Most of us like step-by-step processes. There are four steps to optimizing the patient experience in a dental practice.

1. **Measurement:** You can't improve the score if you don't know the score. Therefore, you'll need to know your baseline score for your practice in two areas.

   □ Telephone: mystery calls to assess the telephone customer experience are objective, credible, and effective. Dental Team Performance measures thousands of calls for dental practices. On a scale of 1 to 100, the average score is 71 (a C-). You'll want your score to be 90 or above.

- In-office: patient surveys, if delivered correctly, are far more effective and accurate than online surveys. You control the survey questions, you will receive a much larger number of surveys, and you will receive a much better cross-section of your patients, too.

These two scores will illuminate the experience your patients have with you and your team. Remember people do business with people. This is your primary focus. A nice and clean facility matters; a coffee maker and bottled water in a minifridge are nice; and artwork is pleasant. But the main thing is the main thing. Focus on the human element. I've seen plenty of incredibly beautiful and well-appointed dental offices with patient experience scores that are dismal. Remember, it's about the people experience.

Create an environment in your practice that enhances how your patients feel about you and your team. Perfection is impossible, but being consistently exceptional is expected. Your patients will reward you again and again.

2. **Protocols: the *what*.** Once you know your score, it's time to think through every people connection that patients will experience in your practice after they walk through the front door. From the greeting by a front desk professional

to meeting a clinician and a doctor and then back to the front desk for check-out or financial arrangements, the people connections need to be optimal. Map the people connections for prophy, operatory, and emergency patients. Discuss and note every action that will improve how patients feel. Put it in writing.

3. **Skills (communications): the *how*.** Now you and your team know the score and you all know what to do to improve the score. The third step is to know *how* to do the *what* in order to improve the score. We have experience in this area, having served more than 30,000 employees. Written guidelines and a couple of short coaching sessions will improve the results significantly. The reason is simple. Most team members already know the basics. But there is no focus in the practice to achieve a high level of patient experience and there is no accountability. Therefore, measurement (see step 1 above) provides the baseline accountability; protocols (see step 2 above) set the expectations; and skills (see step 3 above) provide the know-how. It continues to amaze me how team members immediately improve their performance with steps 1, 2, and 3. But wait, there's one more step: the grand finale!

4. **Reward:** What's in it for me? Reward comes in two favorite flavors: recognition and money. A reasonable scoop of both is best. Recognition is free. Unfortunately, we leaders have a tendency to notice things that go wrong in our businesses. The guilty party is then corrected. We also have a tendency to *not* catch our team members doing things exceptionally well and, therefore, we don't look for opportunities to personally recognize our team members'

efforts and results. The vast majority of your team members want to please you. They work hard to meet your expectations. Be aware of your team members' efforts and results. A little praise goes a long way. I mentioned the law of reciprocity earlier. When you recognize the efforts of one or more of your team members, guess what happens? The team member will have a strong tendency to repeat the action that attracted the recognition. Reciprocation at its finest! It's human nature and you can't fool Mother Nature. Catch your team members doing something right, including creating consistently exceptional experiences for your patients.

□ The financial reward can be individualized or designed as a team reward. There are situations when an individual reward can be justified for the patient experience, but remember the original objective: consistently exceptional patient experiences. The key word, *consistently*, suggests that every team member be engaged in delivering the goods. If not, it's inconsistent. Therefore, our best results with clients occur when the financial reward is based on team performance.

□ You should have two objective measurements from which to design an incentive reward: telephone mystery call scores and internal patient survey scores. Your baseline score for both should set the bar for improving the score.

□ As soon as you know your baseline scores, I recommend creating three levels of incentive reward, with the first level being easily achievable. This will motivate your team members to reach the second and third levels.

Use personal recognition, when earned, to reward team members for subjective patient experience performance.

Keeping this key strategy top of mind is very important for you and your team. Whether you are in morning huddles or team meetings, make the patient experience a talking point at least weekly. Remind the team of the baseline scores, the most recent scores, the protocols, and the skills, and thank your team members for all that they do.

As discussed, the patient experience is the number-one unique value that you and your team can deliver. Any practice can make this happen, but few dentist/owners understand the massive long-term benefits. I hope you understand them. Your patients will reward you in many ways, all of which are very beneficial for your practice. It's the right thing to do for your patients and your practice. Then, the results can accelerate. So, first things first! Measure your patient experience score via the telephone and in-office.

—— CASE STUDY ——
Lynsey Brown, DMD, and Team

Dr. Brown balances production optimization while maintaining a quality family life with her husband and twin boys. With a planned workweek of three and a half days, she and her team members minimize open appointments on her schedule and the hygienist's schedule. They optimize case completion and their patient experience scores are off-the-chart high. Therefore, production, collections, and profit are consistently maximized.

As a part of Dr. Brown's strategic plan, the patient experience was measured with telephone mystery calls asking questions about daily, basic activities. The original baseline score for the practice was 71 (C-). Therefore, the baseline score/measurement was set. Protocols and skills were developed and coaching followed. With the telephone mystery calls continuing quarterly, ample time was devoted to improve the results. Kudos to the team, because the results not only improved, they were spectacular. The team graduated from a 71 (C-) to 85, 99, 84, 99, and 97. It doesn't get any better!

Now you know how to improve the patient experience in your practice:

1. Know your score to improve your score.
2. Establish the protocols to improve the score.
3. Learn and coach the communication skills to improve the score.
4. Reward your team for improvements in the score.

At Dental Team Performance, we help dentists/owners improve the patient experience in their practice by measuring their baseline score, helping them establish their protocols, delivering and coaching communication skills, and helping them design the best incentive plan to reward performance. Discover how by visiting www.whydtp.com or call 800-943-9638.

CHAPTER TWO

STRATEGIC PLANNING TO FOCUS

STRATEGY #2

YOUR STRATEGIC GAME PLAN DICTATES YOUR RESULTS

"Failing to plan is planning to fail."
—Sir Winston Churchill

As a speaker and continuing education lecturer serving thousands of dentists, I'll often ask our dentist attendees, "Do you own a written strategic plan designed to optimize production and collections for your practice?" Only one dentist has ever answered yes (in Charleston, South Carolina). That's amazing! How can business owners possibly maximize revenue, minimize expenses, and optimize profit without a well-thought-out plan? They can't!

So, what is a strategic plan and why should you not leave home without one? Let's start by defining what a strategic plan isn't:

- It isn't a program or product.
- It isn't about dentistry.
- It isn't a quick-fill form to submit for third-party review.
- It isn't a financial analysis.

- It has nothing to do with comparing your practice numbers or percentiles to other practices, nationally, regionally, or even in your market area.
- It isn't about finding every little thing that you think needs to be improved.

Here is what a strategic plan is:

- It's a comprehensive analysis for the operational health of a dental practice.
- It's about the patient experience—efficiently and effectively serving patients' needs.
- It's about team members, their buy-in and commitment to team performance.
- It's about finding your main focus, just three to five key production drivers.
- It's about what to do and how to do it.
- It's about a step-by-step process to execute your plan.
- It can be maintained by you and your team.
- It's objectively measurable and predictive of significant and sustainable results.
- It's about optimizing production, collections, and profit, and minimizing stress.

As I've noted, we have served more than 1,200 companies in 44 states. Show me an organization that owns and follows a comprehensive strategic plan and I'll show you an organization in which:

- team members are committed and happy;
- customers/patients are advocates;
- production is consistently in the top 10 percent of the organization's peers.

That just about sums it up. Isn't that what you want? It's just common sense. Without a well-thought-out plan, how can dentist/owners possibly *optimize team performance* that best serves their patients' needs, clinically and emotionally? They can't! Therefore, if they can't optimize team performance, they can't optimize production, collections, and profit.

As noted in the Introduction, I didn't invite myself into the dental industry. My next-door neighbor and good friend simply asked me a few questions on a Saturday morning over the fence between our homes. I offered to discuss his situation as an outsider of the industry. We met at his office the following week for lunch. After looking at his basic data and listening to the details of his situation, I suggested he call one of his existing advisors and initiate a strategic plan for two reasons, 1) to determine the best course of action to grow his practice, and 2) to determine what not to do that could undermine his best intentions. Then, he asked me to define a strategic plan. Hmmm! Surely, this smart and successful dentist had conducted some form of comprehensive business plan to grow his practice. Nope. So, I asked, "Kevin, what do your peers do? Do they conduct any form of strategic planning?" Negative! To make matters worse, none of his advisers were in the strategic planning business. Oh my, what to do now? My team and I were flying all over the country every week, serving our clients, and I really didn't have time to get involved. But I made time because you'll never find a nicer, more caring, more professional, and more deserving human than my neighbor (and dentist) Kevin Alexander. By the way, Kevin's practice had done quite well, despite not having a strategic plan. But that was before the Great Recession!

Over the next couple of weeks, I met with Kevin to make sure I clearly understood the culture of his practice, his business needs, and the information I had already gathered. I then met with each of his team members. I collected more fact-facts and feeling-facts. Next, as I've done for years, I converted my expandable file folder of his information to a written comprehensive strategic plan. A week later, I delivered Kevin's strategic plan in a two-hour meeting. While Kevin was quite comfortable with knowing the traditional industry benchmarks, he was surprised to learn that data we had repurposed from his software told a completely different story about his practice. He could clearly see the four key production drivers (KPDs) that mattered most to his practice and the production gaps in each, and he was beginning to understand how team performance in each KPD would add significant and sustainable production. Since I had gone this far, our team implemented the plan for his practice beginning in January 2009, at the height of the recession. By the end of 2009, Kevin's practice had amassed a record year of production and collections. Since then, we've updated his strategic plan every year, and assisted Kevin in assuring that the plan has been executed as mutually agreed by his team members and him. The results are as follows: record years in 2009, 2010, 2011, 2012, and 2013, collectively increasing collections by 42 percent. While Kevin has become quite the leader, his team members deserve a great deal of credit for being a part of the solutions every step of the way. They committed to the plan and consistently perform exceptionally well.

A major part of designing a strategic plan is to make sure that it includes self-motivating initiatives for the team, specific to the critical pieces of the plan.

Since Kevin's first year of success with his

strategic plan, word has traveled quickly. As of the end of 2013, we've served 186 practices with a comprehensive strategic plan and another 163 practices with specific and tailored production drivers.

So, how important is strategic planning? Very! It's essential. From dentists opening a new practice or buying a practice to dentists who have practiced for 10, 20, or 30 years, a strategic plan is the instigator, facilitator, and accelerator of team performance and production. For dentists thinking about transitioning, a strategic plan should be in place to maximize production and collections prior to selling to earn more now and increase the purchase price. Think about it. A practice that is demonstrating production growth is going to command a bigger price that one that isn't. Recently, a client's collections increased by $186,000 in the nine months prior to the sale, which added $123,000 to the sale price. Combined, that's over $300,000 in increased value, in a short period of time.

DEBUNKING MYTHS

1. "I don't have time to do this!" Actually, it's a time saver. Based on our experiences with hundreds of practices, there is an abundance of time and effort wasted on inefficient and unproductive initiatives, projects, and programs. Four to six hours invested to own a strategic plan can save your team, and you, hundreds of hours per year of unproductive work and limited results.

2. "This sounds too complicated!" If you've never done it, I agree. This is not a do-it-yourself project. But it's no different from outsourcing your tax preparation to a CPA. Just get it done! Engage a known and proven strategic planner who specializes in dental practices. Remember,

though, you aren't looking for a third-party evaluation. A comprehensive strategic plan goes deep into the why, what, when, where, who, and how. The end objective is to have a plan that is ready to execute and one that your team buys into. It is also a plan you can expect to create significant and sustainable production. When you need help with your computers and software, you call your tech expert. When you need help with your website, you call a web guru. When your toilet doesn't flush, you call your plumber. When you need a strategic plan, you call a known and proven strategic planner with one objective: to create the best strategic plan for your practice, your team, and your patient mix.

3. "My practice is too small (or too large) for a strategic plan!" Are you running a for-profit business or not? If you are truly happy and content with your practice just as it is, then strategic planning is not for you. If you are not truly happy and content with your practice, then the only way to get happy and content is to plan your way to achieve contentment and happiness.

4. "John, I just need more new patients and everything will be just fine!" Okay, but is the best solution for your practice really about more new patients or is it really about filling the schedules (hygiene and doctor appointments)? Be careful with your answer. If it's the latter, then there are easier, less costly, and more productive ways to fill the schedule than relying solely on trying to attract more new patients. If you have 50 or more open appointments per month on your hygiene schedule and 30 or more per month per doc, good luck filling the schedules with only new patients. Your

strategic plan should include finding the most efficient and effective methods to fill the schedules—to minimize open appointments. Period.

5. "I know what to do. I've attended the best practice management meetings and boot camps in the country, and I've had three consultants come to my office. But, for some reason, we just don't seem to know *how to do it*!" I hear you! But a baseball team has nine players. All are baseball players, but each has a different specialty. The same is true of football players and consultants. Each one has his or her own specialty or niche set of skills. Sure, there can be obvious needs. But the embedded issues in dental practices that deter the dentist/owners from achieving the potential of their practice can be far deeper than the obvious. The real issues could be right under your nose, but not visible. Dentists can be too close to the day-to-day action to see the reality. Further, dentists' business decisions are often based on their emotions or a team member's emotions (or all of them), instead of on facts and logic. The best decisions can be made when the information is as accurate as possible, adequate baseline measurements exist, and there is a logical path for the team to take to improve the measurements.

— THE REALITY: A CASE STUDY —
University General Dentistry
Drs. Stan Turnipseed, David Nelson and William Roe

Partners Stan Turnipseed, DMD, and William Roe, DMD, and their associate David Nelson, DMD, like most other dentists, wanted to grow their practice. They already knew that there was a big gap

Dr. David S. Turnipseed, DMD   Dr. David D. Nelson, DMD   Dr. William D. Roe DDS, DMD

between their current production and collections compared to where they should be. Too many no-shows and cancellations and not enough new patients and referrals were taking their toll on production. Those were the surface issues. They had enjoyed limited success with prior do-it-yourself solutions, and a nationally known consulting firm. What to do? Thanks to a suggestion from their supply rep, they attended a seminar on strategic planning for dentists. I was the presenter and they requested our help to create a strategic plan for their practice.

As a part of the comprehensive analysis, five key production drivers were discovered, including measurable before-and-after production gaps for each. The written strategic plan included specific tactics to close the gaps and increase production in each KPD, plus steps to implement the improvements in each. With the plan delivered, Stan and William had three choices. They could do nothing with the plan, execute all or part of the plan internally, or partner with Dental Team Performance. They chose the latter.

Fast forward. Open doc appointments have been reduced by 16 percent. Open hygiene appointments have been reduced by 38 percent. The patient experience scores have increased by 24 percent. One KPD was more important than any other: Case Acceptance to Completion. Since their average operatory "case" production per patient was a bit over $1,000, small but critical improvements in this KPD amounted to the biggest share of the increase in overall production. All in, by planning the growth of their practice strategically, University General Dentistry has increased production by an average of 20 percent since late 2011. That's what a strategic plan should accomplish: focus, team performance, and significant and sustainable results!

> *We are like most dentists. We just want to serve our patients as best as we can, clinically and professionally. And we want our team members to demonstrate a high level of service and care for our patients. Yes, we want to run a productive practice, too. John and Lisa at Dental Team Performance invested the time to get to know our practice. They evaluated and analyzed our practice over several weeks to make sure we owned a strategic plan focused on the main things and to make sure we could execute the plan. When John presented our plan to us, it was clear that he knew what our wants and needs were (along with a few things we didn't know we wanted or needed), and he knew how to help us achieve them. We are beyond pleased with the outcome, especially the sustainability of the results.*

—Stan Turnipseed, DMD, Managing Partner

Dentists *plan* their business and personal taxes, investments and insurance, and vacations. Why?

- To get the biggest benefits
- To minimize stress
- To minimize costs
- To prevent future financial problems
- To maximize the return on investment
- To maximize pleasure and minimize pain

Then, why not plan for the economic engine that makes everything else possible?

Comprehensive Means Wide and Deep

I've mentioned three to five key production drivers. Unfortunately, most of us have a very long to-do list of things that can improve our businesses. Some are priorities, but are they the best priorities? Others are more of a when-I-get-to-it list. Focusing on three to five main things that generate the biggest impact on production makes sense. It's doable. It eliminates, or at least reduces, distractions. If we try to focus on the entire list, very little gets improved. Know your three to five big things. Know before you go! When you know your three to five key production drivers, you can plan to improve each. Therefore, make your wide list but narrow the focus to the three to five that matter most.

Now, go deep! Let's say that in the comprehensive analysis part of the strategic planning process, I note that a practice has two full-time hygienists averaging 63 open appointments per month. We all know that keeping the hygiene schedule as full as possible every day is very important, but it's also a problem for most practices. Assuming that you agree with me that 63 is way too high (33 would be better), before we look for solutions, let's evaluate what is causing so many open appointments. If you don't know the cause (the *why*), then finding the best solution would be like throwing darts blindfolded. Is it too many no-shows and cancellations? If so, why? Is it too few new patients and referrals? If so, why? How about the patient experience score? Why is the score 71 when it should be 90-plus? How about recall/recare? The recall area, alone, requires its own deep-dive analysis. Who does recall? Where is it done? When is it done? How many calls are made? How many appointments are made? What's the communication skill level? Where are we cultivating the names to call? A strategic plan will show why a result is what it is. Without a comprehensive exam that finds the cause of the problems, there is no realistic way to solve the problems.

For example, I see practices where any team member with an extra few minutes of time is expected to help with recall. It's all hands on deck to fill the schedule. Grab the quick-fill list and dial away. But wait! Why would you waste a perfectly good name on the recall list with a team member who has less than adequate telephone skills? Are the calls made at the front desk while patients are checking in and checking out, and while the telephone is ringing? In that example, recall needs to improve, but what are the variables that affect success or failure with each outbound call? The foundational essence of strategic planning is to know the facts before jumping to conclusions. I want to know what is causing the big number of open appointments. When I know the reasons, then I can craft a doable plan for the specific team in the specific practice. The best solutions can be quite different for a team in practice A compared to a team in practice B. Because of the variables, the best solutions should be tailored to the causes of the problems.

I'll look at every angle to determine how to improve no-shows, cancellations, new patients (NPs), referrals and recall, and, maybe, a few other opportunities that are discovered in the strategic planning process. Then, I'll plan the process *with* the designated team, not just *for* the designated team. Remember people buy into what they help create. Tell them what to do and you are asking for push-back and limited, if not zero, results. Team members want easier and better ways to do their job and they don't want to think, "This is just more work." Engage team members to create the best solutions. Buy-in happens, and then results happen!

Engaging a dental practice strategic planner to help you develop your plan is smart, because the right planner can have a huge impact on the success of a dental practice, save the owner a lot of future lost production, and save a lot of future stress and frustration. But unfortunately, strategic planners get tossed into the heap of those consultants. It's perfectly normal for the parents of the bride to engage a wedding planner, but for some reason, not to engage a strategic planner for the economic engine that pays for the wedding. While every industry has a few not-so-adept members, there are plenty of top-notch consultants who do amazing things for dentists. The strategic planner is going to make your team members' jobs easier, help them to perform at a higher level in the key production drivers, and help you achieve your goals—likely going far beyond your goals.

In the next chapter, I'll discuss key production drivers in detail. For now, the focus is on the depth and breadth of strategic planning, especially when it's done the right way. And it has to be done the right way, with empirical facts and a clear understanding of the causes of the problems. Because the true causes of the problems are rarely identified without a plan, it is quite common for dentists to purchase cookie-cutter CDs, DVDs, group coaching programs, and even off-the-shelf solutions. Look, plenty of really good content is offered by a bunch of excellent consultants. The question, however, isn't the quality of the content; it's whether or not the content is the best solution for your problem. If not, it's wasted time and money. You might say, "But it's only $187 or $650. Why not try it?" Here's why! Team members are sick and tired of being guinea pigs for cookie-cutter, piecemeal products and programs. They can smell it coming a mile away. If you show up on Monday morning with the newest hope-and-change panacea to solve a problem in your practice, rest assured your team will find every excuse why it will not work. Therefore, they can make sure it doesn't. Flip the motivator to a positive for them!

Strategic planning involves the team members as much as, if not more than, the doctor. No solution should be introduced to the team without their input. That's just common sense. Remember this. When the team sees how a solution works on the front-end before it becomes a to-do task, the solution has a high degree of achieving what you want to achieve on the back-end: Results.

—— CASE STUDY ——————————————
Stuart Atkinson, DMD

Eighteen months ago, I received a call from a supply rep. Her dentist customer was looking to improve the operational systems and processes in his practice. While he had purchased CAD/CAM technology, and intraoral cameras, and had updated his practice management software, something was obviously missing. In the last few years, production and collections had remained stagnant. My friend called me with the dentist's permission to contact him to discuss his situation. After three attempts to connect, I assumed he wasn't motivated to meet. A year later, we met at one of my seminars and we scheduled a private conversation. The conversation and issues were similar to many I've experienced with dentist/owners:

- Not sure if we have the right processes.

- Not sure I'm doing my part to manage my team.
- Not sure if we have the right people skills.
- Can't determine why collections are slow, and lower than they should be.
- Can't seem to get the schedule booked for maximum production.
- Have way too many cancellations and no-shows.
- How are other dentists growing in the down economy?

Sound familiar?

Over the next few weeks, Stuart and I explored the depth and breadth of the issues to help us both better understand his situation: what he understands is happening in specific areas of his practice, what he doesn't know is happening, what he wants to happen in specific areas, and his big picture goals. I interviewed each team member one-on-one. I collected 13 performance numbers specific to his practice's performance. After all of the information and data was collected, reviewed, and mapped in a skeleton strategy, I had another conversation with Stuart to make sure my overarching assessment was on track. I transferred all of the information to a 15-page comprehensive strategic plan. Next, we set aside two hours to discuss the plan. Stuart's strategic plan included four key production drivers, with detailed explanations of why they are important, the performance gaps in each, the new production opportunities in each, how to measure and implement each, and how to recognize and reward the team for achieving each.

Knowing all of the facts and knowing the team members' abilities via the interviews makes it relatively easy to predict the overall increase in production over a specific period of time. I noted in his plan that, conservatively, he should be able to increase production by $12,000 to $18,000 per month within six months, and sustain that level month-over-month. These results would happen if he were to follow the step-by-step process described in his plan. With his plan completed, delivered, and crystal clear to him, he asked if we would help with the implementation of it, which we did.

The result over the first five months of our engagement: collections increased by 22.48 percent.

Strategic planning isn't a program or a product. It's a necessity to optimize the performance of any business.

A 22.48 percent increase in collections in five months doesn't happen unless a plan is developed and executed. The biggest problem isn't the creation of the plan; it's waiting to do it.

Your team members dictate your production! Their buy-in and commitment is priceless. Make it happen!

Your team members dictate your production! Their buy-in and commitment is priceless. Make it happen!

At Dental Team Performance we help dentist/owners create strategic plans for their practices by helping them find their three to five key production drivers that matter most. Built around the key motivating factors that affect patients' behaviors and maximizing team members' buy-in and commitment, a strategic plan is about the facts and the people that affect the facts. When team members win and patients win, the dentist wins. Discover how you can own a strategic plan for your practice by visiting www.whydtp.com or calling 800-943-9638.

CHAPTER THREE

FILL THE SCHEDULE TO PRODUCTION

STRATEGY #3

If you want to maximize production and collections, a focused mindset is critically important. Too many to-do items diminish the team members' and doctor's ability to optimize the results in any plan, much less in the area of key production drivers that matter most. Frankly, some of your long list of to-do items will roll up under one or more of the key production drivers anyway.

Another mindset reality is that someone has to take the necessary actions to improve the key-production-driver baseline numbers. That can sound like more work. Admittedly, there are a few instances when your strategic plan will call for something new to be implemented. But most often, the action will be in something your team member is already doing. The improved method will simply be an easier and better way to achieve better results with less effort, time, and frustration. Thus, there is less work, not more.

"How am I going to get my team motivated, and stay motivated, to do this stuff? John, it's hard enough to get the basics accomplished in our practice. This sounds like a foreign language to me and it will sound the same to my team too." I've heard all sorts of excuses why this or that will not happen. For sure, if you keep doing what you are doing, you'll keep getting what you are getting. So, hang in there with me. Where there is a will, there is a way. So, if you have the will to improve your practice for the benefit of your team, your patients, and yourself, then it's doable and much easier than you think. The key is self-motivation! By the end of this chapter, you'll see how it can happen.

Motivation! As a teenager, I remember my dad saying, "If I had a dime for every time I've heard [fill in the blank], I would be rich." Well, in honor of my dad, if I had a dollar (inflation) for every time I've been asked, "John, can you help motivate my team," I would be rich too. Motivational speeches and rah-rah presentations are inspirational for the moment. But in 24 hours these attempts to motivate are but a memory. Nothing happens. Nothing improves.

Self-Motivation. Now, that's the ticket. It comes from within, it's personal, and it's lasting. So, how are we going to pull this off, when it's been a mystery for millions of business owners just like you? Frankly, I've already given you the four-step formula. But I'll explain it again in the context of this chapter so you can apply the formula to your practice.

It's hard to motivate a team with a concept such as, "We need to work harder to improve our production," or "If we achieve our production/collection goals, everyone will get a bonus," or "let's work smarter, not harder." Team members can easily translate those statements to "You [the dentist] want to make more money, but we haven't had a raise in three years and we received only two bonus checks last year." When team members are asked to produce more, they rarely connect the dots of what they do all day to improving production. Conversely, when they are asked to focus on what they do day-in and day-out, specific to the main strategies that drive production, they can see it, believe it, and improve the results. Here's a simple example: Ask a team member to improve production. She will ask you how you want her to do it. Your answer could be an hour-long dialogue and still not help the team member do what you want her to do. Now, ask your team member to improve the results of recall. She may ask you how, and your answer should be easy to explain with specifics, because your strategic plan will cover improving recall results from front to back. While recall isn't a key production driver, it's a piece of minimizing open appointments, which is a KPD for most practices. Is your team member self-motivated? Not yet. But she knows what to do and how to do it. As you understand the four steps, you'll see self-motivation come to life. It's fun to watch it happen when team members make it happen!

As I explain the four steps, you'll also see how everyone will be on the same mission, because the four steps are all about team performance with a big focus on your patients and the team members. Get this mindset and you are off to the races.

Let's take minimizing open appointments as a KPD example to explain the four-step formula and how self-motivation is achievable.

- Step 1: There is a specific measurement for hygiene open appointments that is easy to see and it's completely transparent. Looking back at the schedule over a three-month period, anyone can count the number of open appointments (OA) and then divide the total by three for a monthly average. Everybody agrees. Unquestionable. Got it!

- Step 2: Rather than "tell" your team what you think they need to do to improve the OA number, someone needs to engage the team, acting as a facilitator to help the team and doctor find the best protocols to reduce hygiene OA. Don't tell. Engage. The protocols are the "what to do" and the team members will buy in and commit to what they help create.

- Step 3: Since reducing OA is about the team and the patients, what are the communication skills needed to optimize the agreed-on protocols that will improve the measurement?
- Step 4: When steps 2 and 3 are executed and the measurement improves, reward the team for achieving the improvement.

This magic potion will reduce hygiene OA. You and your team will have a specific goal for a specific need, and everyone will be on the same page with regard to what to do, how to do it, and the reward for doing it.

So, identify the current score, define what (protocols) we need to improve the score, define the skills (communication) to execute the protocols, and reward the team when the score is improved. Expectations have been set and communicated, and now the dentist has every reason to expect improved results. Done!

Don't work harder; perform better!

That's as good as it gets for creating self-motivation!

Don't work harder; perform better!

STRATEGY #3: FILL THE SCHEDULE TO PRODUCTION

Your strategic plan may identify hygiene open appointments as a key production driver. Your plan may also identify doc open appointments as a KPD. Or both may be combined.

I recently delivered a strategic plan to a dentist in Atlanta who had 28 open hygiene appointments per month for two full-time hygienists. I'm sure that their 28 can be reduced, but not by much. Zero is not possible. In designing the strategies and tactics for the doctor's strategic plan, I made it clear to him that putting on a full-court press to reduce hygiene open appointments was not the best use of his team's time and efforts. A few tactics and protocol improvements will minimize the 28, while we deploy team performance on other KPDs that can drive bigger results faster. On the other hand, had this practice been averaging 60 hygiene OA per month, the focus would be heightened. The point: You want to invest your time, talent, and efforts in the KPDs that have the biggest impact on production. Make sense?

Generally, we've found that there are five core tactics that minimize hygiene open appointments. None of the tactics on their own will minimize OA on the hygiene schedule.

Incremental improvements in *each* of the five tactics are easy to achieve and will garner impressive results. Read that last sentence one more time. Combined, the results are impressive. Don't fall into the mindset that you have to be a genius to solve a problem or you have to work harder. The word *work* is about doing things. I hear doctors and team members say, "We need to work smarter, not harder." I disagree. How about this: "We need to perform better"! Working harder or smarter may not improve anything, but performing better in a specific tactic that improves a key performance driver hits the target in the sweet spot. That's being smarter, too!

Let's use the same example mentioned earlier: minimize open appointments in recall for overdue prophy, a need for most practices. Prior to your strategic plan, recall was conducted at the front desk. But patients can be checking in and checking out, and the telephone can be ringing off the hook. Plus, patients might need a treatment plan review and a financial estimate. At times, it can resemble chaos.

With few exceptions, the recall guru never knows when his or her recall efforts will be interrupted. Wouldn't you agree that lack of focus and lots of interruptions can have a negative effect on recall results? Then, if there is a better alternative that achieves better results, why not use it?

Recall has to get done! You just dialed Mrs. Jones' telephone number to schedule her for her missed prophy appointment and she answers her phone at the same time that Mr. Tucker comes to the front desk to check out and pay. Now the other telephone line is ringing, and Mrs. Coleman comes to the front desk needing a financial estimate. With two team members at the front desk, some of this insanity can be calmed. Nevertheless, you are trying to fill the hygiene schedule with lots of distractions. What to do?

It simply isn't reasonable to believe that any human being can focus on recall and achieve the best results while negotiating day-to-day, hour-by-hour distractions. I remember the third practice we ever served. A quite capable and experienced front-desk-team member, Susan, made 83 recall telephone calls on the day I conducted the team members' interviews for their strategic plan. Susan scheduled three appointments out of 83 calls and was thrilled with the results. The dentist had no idea so much time was devoted to recall and so few appointments were actually being scheduled. No one, in 13 years, had stepped back from the chaos to evaluate the results.

It's not a matter of finding fault. It's a matter of determining why the problem exists, finding the best solutions, and getting focused. A month later, Susan was using a private area in 30-minute increments twice per day, while another team member managed the front desk in these short time periods. Susan quadrupled her results. She spent less time to increase results by 400 percent! Bingo! Who wins in this improved protocol? Everyone! Susan achieved better results in less time and with less stress. She is also self-motivated to repeat the results, over and over again, because she knows the importance of filling the schedule. Now she has a protocol, and the skills to do it. Mrs. Jones received the attention and care she deserved on the telephone. Mr. Tucker checked out promptly. Mrs. Coleman not only received her financial arrangement but she also scheduled the treatment (TX). Conducting recall at the front desk can diminish results in other areas.

Then, there is Dr. Samson in this example. Over the next 90 to 120 days, several other tactics were implemented to minimize the 68-per-month average of open appointments. The average monthly OA dropped below 35 per month, consistently. That's an additional 33 seen appointments per month and an increase in hygiene production of 22 percent! Also, Dr. Samson had more than 35 additional prophy checks, and diagnosed more dentistry, which added more treatments, which added another $8,300 per month to doc production. That's the cascading effect of performing better in one protocol, in one tactic, and in one key production driver.

The moral of the story is rather simple:

Get focused on a key production driver. Get self-motivated with measurements, protocol, skills, and reward, and go!

I mentioned the following chart in Chapter One, but it's a good time to take another quick look at some of the results of using the five core tactics that we've found to be effective in minimizing hygiene OA. And don't forget. They're easy!

Get focused on a key production driver. Get self-motivated with measurements, protocol, skills, and reward, and go!

THE RESULTS OF OPTIMIZING THE PATIENT EXPERIENCE

✓	No-shows:	2 fewer per week
✓	Cancellations:	2 fewer per week
✓	New patients:	1 more per week
✓	Referrals:	1 more per week
✓	Recare/recall:	2 more per week
	Total per week:	8 more patients seen per week
	Total per month:	32 more patients seen per month
	Total results:	$10,000+/- in new production per month

First, I know you want a quick fix. But don't forget that most consumers (patients included) behave and make decisions, to a large extent, based on how they feel about your practice, every touch point, every person, and every connection. The level of the results in your practice will mirror the level of the patient experience that is delivered in your practice, consistently. The same is true with specific action tactics, such as recall. It is human nature and you can't gloss over it. So, you might want to take another tour through Chapter One. Improving the patient experience is foundational to improving anything and everything that matters.

New Patients

Okay, back to other specific tactics to minimize open appointments: increasing new-patient numbers and attracting more referrals. First, let's remember that filling the schedule is achieved by five tactics, at least. And remember it's easy. Don't do something that *might* make a difference. Do something that can *succeed*. In other words, evaluate the results before you proceed. With regard to new patients, there is a critical component to consider. How many *active patients* do you have?

Your active patient number is a factor in determining what needs to be done to improve your new patient numbers. Here's a general rule of thumb. A solo GP with 2,500-plus active patients, seeing 30 new patients (code 0150) per month should *not* invest lots of time and money to attract 10 to 15 more new patients per month. The schedule should be filled, primarily, by the active patients via improving recall, no-shows, cancellations, and referrals. Let's face it, your active patients already know, like, and trust you and your team, but new patients do not know, like, and trust you. They are neophytes to your practice.

Every business has to attract new customers in order to survive and to thrive. First things first! Compare the real return on investment of appointing active patients versus acquiring new patients. It's not even close. Scheduling active patients has a low, or no, cost, and active patients are much more likely to show up for an appointment. New patients cost more to acquire (schedule), have a higher rate of no-show and cancellation than do active patients, and have a lower rate of case acceptance than do active patients. Think about the best use of your resources and your team members. There's only so much time, talent, effort, and money. Make sure you maximize your results with your active patients. Acquiring new patients, other than referrals, requires marketing. Remember the name of the game is to fill the schedule. If it can be done with active patients, do it. If marketing is needed to acquire new patients, think about a mini-strategic plan for marketing.

Also, let's be clear. The telephone is already ringing a lot with prospective patient calls. Here are two questions for you: How many incoming prospective patient calls does your practice receive each month? How many of the incoming prospective patient calls are converted to new patients? The point: The opportunity to appoint more new patients is available every day, now. If you don't know the score, it's difficult to improve the score. Measure your number of incoming prospective patient calls and conversions to new patients. Three months of numbers will give you a reasonable average. This is the best first step to improving your new patient numbers. Money on the table: you'll increase your new patient numbers simply by measuring (keeping score of) the number of incoming prospective new patient calls and the number of those calls that result in a new patient appointment.

Now you know your baseline score (the measurement). Next, develop the protocols, skills, and reward to improve the baseline score. When you have optimized the conversion rate from incoming prospective patient calls, you will know whether or not you need or want to attract more new patients. Otherwise, it doesn't make sense to increase the number of incoming calls if the current incoming calls are not converted to new patients at an acceptable level.

Referrals

Over the years, many people have asked me to refer my clients to them. Occasionally, the value such a person can provide to my client or group of clients makes sense. In those cases, I have to determine the best way to make the introduction. I feel uncomfortable doing that unless the value that my client will receive will be extraordinary. I use this personal story to make a point. I do not like to be asked to refer my clients to others. And patients don't like to be asked to refer their friends to their dentist. Do you like to be asked to refer a friend to someone? Probably not. Then, it's probably not a good idea to ask your team members to ask your patients to refer their friends to your practice.

However, referrals should happen at a high rate. During the strategic planning process, when I see referrals representing less than 50 percent of the average monthly new patient number, I know we have work to do. But how? This is going to sound like a broken record to you. Create an environment in your practice that generates patient advocates, consistently. The more the better! Look at it from your own perspective, not mine. You have done business with people and/or companies that you have felt "just get it." At every step of the engagement, they get it right. They are very professional and nothing they do sends a negative signal to you. They surprise you with something extra that tells you they care, that they are paying attention to needs you didn't even know you had. That's the consummate customer/patient experience.

What happens? You tell everybody you know how wonderfully this person or company treats you. It's human nature, the law of reciprocity, again. You do something nice for me and I do something nice for you. That's a referral machine. And the best part is that it's free!

Let's say you have 2,000 active patients. What an incredible base from which to create a referral mecca. It isn't rocket science. I discussed this in Strategy #1: The Patient Experience. When you get a chance, read that chapter (Chapter One) again.

No-Shows and Cancellations

Why do people not show up for a scheduled appointment? Why do people cancel appointments? Admittedly, I forgot an appointment with Kevin a few years ago. I just forgot to pay attention to my appointment calendar that morning. When Nickole called me, I was mortified and apologetic. It hasn't happened again. I have had to reschedule a few prophy appointments over the years when, frankly, it was the only time one of my clients could meet with me. I, of all people who know dentists' time is valuable and blocked for the benefit of us patients, occasionally can't show up for an appointment. So, the point is zero no-shows and cancellations are impossible to avoid.

I'll not bore you with the obvious solutions you already employ, such as your quick-fill list. Likely, you already clearly communicate with your patients, telling them that you have reserved time just for them. Perhaps you have a cancelled/no-show appointment fee. I'm asked frequently about my opinion of cancellation fees. Personally, I think they are perfectly fine, as long as the purpose and rules are clearly communicated to all of your patients, periodically, and to the violators every time they miss an appointment. Plus, make sure you post a nicely worded sign at the front desk to communicate the message. Systemic violators can be evaluated to determine whether or not they deserve to be patients of yours because, sadly, some people just don't get it. They have an entitlement mentality and there is no need to expect they will change their behavior. Don't fall into the trap of allowing potential production to justify courting these patients. They could be costing you more than they are worth.

Other than the standard operating procedures noted above, there are a few other techniques to reduce no-shows and cancellations. The three overarching tactics Dental Team Performance has found to minimize these no-shows and cancellations are as follows:

1. The patient experience:

As noted in Chapter One, the better the patient experience, the better the results in everything else. Enough said.

2. Technology-based appointment reminder systems:

You know these systems by name: RevenueWell, Demandforce, SmileReminder (Solutionreach), and Lighthouse 360, among others. The key to the success of these systems is getting them set up properly for your practice and your patient mix. The vendor's standard setup protocols may not be the best setup for your practice. For example, how many times should the system connect with your patients? When should the first message be sent and when should the last message be sent? Are you using the patient's preferred method of connecting or are you blasting e-mails and text messages?

I prefer e-mail, because I will respond promptly. No need to annoy me with a text message. And a telephone call to my cell phone is not a good idea. No need to call my home answering system, either, as I may not check the messages for two weeks. That's me. How about other patients? Don't annoy them! I was meeting with a client who had installed one of these systems a few months ago. While the dentist and I were talking, his office manager walked in and said, "We have a problem. The patient reminder system is continuously sending e-mails and text messages to our patients until they respond, and we are getting calls from irate patients." That's not good! That's a bad patient experience. Obviously, that particular client didn't evaluate the best methods of using the system, and how it could benefit the patients and the practice. The best of intentions gone awry!

Yet these systems can create great experiences if used properly. I'm a big believer in them for several reasons. First, I'm a patient for whom getting an e-mail beats getting a telephone call reminder with the expectation that I have to call back to confirm the appointment. When I receive my e-mail reminder, I click the confirm button on the e-mail and it instantly confirms my appointment in Kevin's practice management software. The second reason I am a believer is my clients' operational health. Think about the big picture. Assume you have 2,000 active patients. Calculate the time it takes them to connect with your practice and confirm the appointment *by telephone*. Anything you can do to eliminate unnecessary work that benefits the patients is smart business. And think of the benefits your practice will receive through the better use of the extra time that was saved. But every practice will have some patients who prefer a telephone call. In those cases, use the telephone!

If you think that all of your patients prefer a telephone call (I hear this often) instead of an e-mail or text message, and therefore you have delayed enrolling in one of these systems, I encourage you to rethink your position. The vast majority of Baby Boomers, most of whom are straddling the young age of 60, are using e-mail, text messages, Facebook, LinkedIn, and other technologies to communicate with family and friends, and business associates. The generations younger than Baby Boomers are even more involved in communicating via technology. If I want to communicate with my three sons, I know to use a text message first. Before my mother passed away at age 84, she was an e-mail guru.

Cost versus benefit—it's a no-brainer! Most of these systems are in the $300-per-month range. A practice can serve patients better and cut call time by 50 percent at a minimum. One of our three-doc practices had a full-time employee who confirmed appointments all day every day via the traditional telephone call method. Then, the practice enrolled in one of these programs. Today the confirmation queen invests roughly 25 percent of her time calling to confirm appointments. We transitioned her to managing unscheduled TX and she is a backup TX coordinator, and a very good one. Along with a focus on one key production driver (coming up) and her new roles, the practice has added $340,000 in collections in 12 months. That's a great example of improving the operational health of a practice, not by working harder but by finding the best efficiencies and performing better.

3. Bi-monthly newsletters:

Attempting to describe a visual tactic in writing that reduces no-shows and cancellations is a bit difficult. First, such a newsletter is a feel-good piece with little, if anything, about dentistry. Second, it's about connecting with your patients. In 2009, before the auto-appointment reminders existed, we used this tactic to minimize cancellations and no-shows, primarily for prophy appointments. We would mail them via USPS to patients with prophy appointments scheduled in the next 60 days—thus bi-monthly. It's easy to crank out a one-page (front and back) newsletter six times per year. But, now, a couple of the auto-appointment reminder programs can attach the newsletter to their delivery system and eliminate the cost of printing, folding, stuffing, and postage, thus significantly reducing the hard copy print and postage expense. No excuses now!

What's the content? Think of the lifestyles and business sections of your local newspaper. They're about people: marriages, people in the news, people in business, and so on. We all like to see who's who. Include a picture of the dentist and the team. When appropriate, give the newsletter a theme: Christmas, New Year's, July 4, Thanksgiving. Have a little fun with it. Your team will love it and your patients will see the human side of you and your team. Dress your team in Santa

Claus hats. Snap a few selfies. Build a template for your newsletter and simply insert your pictures and content. Allow your patients to get in on the action too, but first get their approval in writing (an e-mail will do). We have clients who have included pictures of patients who have written books, caught a big fish, drive an antique car, own businesses, and serve our country through their military service. A feel-good newsletter is powerful.

Think about the patient/business owner for a moment. You are giving your biz owner patients free advertising. Do you think they appreciate you? Keep the size to two pages, front and back—short, sweet, and impactful. With regard to written content, keep it light. Use a little dental trivia. If you feel the urge to mention a clinical subject, make sure it doesn't involve pain. Ortho and whitening are okay. Preventive dentistry works too: oral cancer screening, and so on. Also, use this piece for announcements, such as end-of-year insurance benefits or beginning-of-the-year insurance benefits, and vacation or other office closures. Don't forget to recognize your team members for marriages, childbirths, continuing education of any kind, and so on. Be careful with selling products and special offers. A little goes a long way. Lastly, brand the newsletter with your logo and colors. You get the idea! This newsletter concept is worth a small fortune to you. Be consistent. Bi-monthly is easy. At least, produce a quarterly newsletter!

I'll end this topic with why a newsletter is so important. Earlier, I mentioned how other businesses stay in touch with their customers. Obviously, they want their customers to return to buy more of their products and services. So do you! But there is another factor that doesn't exist in most other businesses. Patients can't find any good reason to go to the dentist except to take care of their dental health. Their mindset is that it takes their valuable time, it might hurt, they may need more dental work, and it costs them money. With that in mind, patients come to the dentist to get their teeth cleaned and schedule an appointment six months in advance for the next appointment. The next time patients hear from their dentist, they get an appointment reminder, which means more time, more pain, more money, and maybe more dental work. Do something to stay in touch with your patients that demonstrates that you care, that it's not always about pain, time, and money. A quarterly, light-hearted newsletter is worth fewer no-shows and cancellations, at the very least.

SUMMARY

We've just covered several proven tactics to fill the schedule, and there's much more I want to share with you regarding the other key production drivers.

1. Get the concept of self-motivation! Everybody can have it. MPSR (measurements, protocols, skills and rewards) fuels it. You can do it for the sake of your patients, your team, and yourself.

2. Find your focus: your key production drivers. Focus on the KPDs that have the biggest opportunity to drive production. Your strategic plan to focus will clearly and metrically identify your three to five KPDs. That's the focus!

3. Fill the schedule to impact production. You have learned cutting-edge tactics that serve hundreds of dentists very productively and very efficiently, month after month. Old-school tactics have run their course. In this economy, with changing consumers' behaviors, results happen when you get in front of the problem, not behind it.

4. Don't drop the ball on MPSR. This is the magic wand and the pixie dust. Moreover, it's the proven business formula that motivates a team to perform to impact a key production driver, including filling the schedule and achieving results beyond compare.

At Dental Team Performance, we help dentist/owners fill the schedule to impact production. It's the economic engine of dental practices and one of the biggest frustrations and stress sources for dentists and team members. Find your focus, reduce the stress and frustration, and fill the schedule. Your patients win, your team members win, and you win. Discover how you can fill the schedule to impact production in your practice by visiting www.whydtp.com, or calling 800-943-9638.

CHAPTER FOUR

CASE ACCEPTANCE TO COMPLETION

STRATEGY #4

Allow me to preface Strategy #4 with a message that has fueled the success of tens of thousands of business leaders, including the most successful private-practice dentists. In essence, the message is about *experience*—not clinical experience but *operational experience*. After my eldest son graduated from orthopedic medical residency and fellowship, it was time for him to find a job. He had to make a decision. Should he focus on finding a private practice or a hospital-owned practice? How should he analyze contracts to fit his best interests, short-term and long-term? He had no experience in either. In fact, like virtually all new doctors, he had no experience in anything related to the business side of medicine. Sound familiar? What did my son do? He did his homework, and more. He wasn't bashful about asking for help. He researched and asked for assistance and help from other doctors (new and experienced). He talked with CPAs, attorneys, and nonmedical business owners and others who could offer advice and counsel. In the end, he made a thoughtful and intelligent decision based on a well-rounded analysis and evaluation. He was strategic!

I know business owners in multiple industries who make a decent living but who will never come close to their potential. They are stuck on what they do today, with no thought about what they could accomplish with their business. They have 10, 15, or 25 years of experience in their niche products and services but do not tap into the successful strategies of the wildly successful. That's a problem in this day and time. They know their products and services but not how to improve the operational aspects of their business: how to hire the best talent, how to maximize team performance, how to outsource and engage a team of professionals to accelerate perfor-mance and revenue, and much more. The most successful business owners learn from those who blaze a trail. They not only find the best recipe for success, they also keep learning.

Having served 30,000+ team members (all of whom I've met at least once), we've certainly been in the teacher role. But make no mistake! We've also been the student, learning new ideas and concepts from our clients. If not for being the teacher, we would never have learned so much, so fast. What if you could learn the inside opera-tional secrets of 500 or more dentists? That would be tremendous. You could be more proactive in directing your practice, preventing problems or issues from ever happening and achieving a higher level of success, more easily and faster. What if you could learn the inside operational secrets of 250 dentists and 250 business owners in other industries? Which grouping of 500 business owners would provide you with the best all-around information to help you? I assume your choice would be the latter, because you would be exposed to and experience a vast array of tried-and-true strategies and tactics that perform extraordinarily well, not only in your industry but in many others too. And many of those strategies you learn from other indus-tries would provide you with a new dimension of knowledge.

EXPERIENCE! NOTHING BEATS EXPERIENCE

The point is that virtually all businesses have the same core needs. We all need more customers. We all need to retain our customers. And we all need customers to use our products and services. Therefore, learn everything you can about successful business owners in the dental field, as well as other industries. Then, you will own the knowledge, expertise, and experience to accelerate success, faster and more easily, while minimizing those expensive and stressful problems and issues that hold you back.

I met a business owner (an architect) several years ago at a mastermind meeting. In our one-on-one meeting, we discussed the length of business experience versus the depth and breadth of business experience. In essence, business owners can have 20 years of experience, but if they are using the same old tactics, they may have only one year of experience, 20 times. Grow the depth and breadth of your operational business knowledge and hand pick those pearls of wisdom from other successful business owners in multiple industries. You'll be a bigger winner sooner, as will your team members and patients. The world of business is moving at warp speed. Think about it! The economy is constantly in motion. Consumers' behaviors change, affecting a landslide of factors in your practice: case completion, no-shows, cancellations, new patients, referrals, and more. And let's not forget your team members. They dictate the production of your practice. What's going on in your practice that negatively and positively affects their performance? What about you? What's your mindset? What do you want to achieve? If you want it, it's yours, but you have to have a plan to achieve it.

This is the reason I recommend dentists join their local chamber of commerce and get active in the chamber's lunch-n-learns and study groups. No, this does not have to affect production time. Dentists who join their chamber meet and learn from other business leaders in other industries. They discover innovative ideas they can use to differentiate their practice from the others. And, by the way, they gain new patients too, the kind of new patients they want. I've been a member of four chambers and several study groups from San Diego to San Mateo to Las Vegas and Birmingham, representing a cross-section of business categories. The knowledge I've gained from these business owners and leaders has been invaluable. In fact, I learned the underlying concept of Strategy #4 (Case Acceptance to Completion) not from the dental industry but from a unique pair—a commercial pipefitting company and a community bank. I know that's an odd couple, but it doesn't matter where you learn new concepts. It just matters that you expand your horizons to gain knowledge from multiple resources.

Also, make sure that you read business-related books. Granted, most business books are about big businesses, but you'll find that many of the underlying concepts are applicable to small businesses, including dental practices. Noted below is a short list of my book recommendations:

- *Good to Great* by Jim Collins
- *The Loyalty Effect* by Frederick Reichheld
- *The Experience Economy* by Joseph Pine II and James Gilmore
- *Great by Choice* by Jim Collins
- *Profit from the Core* by Chris Zook and James Allen
- *The Four Disciplines of Execution* by Chris McChesney and Sean Covey

Each of these will open your eyes to concepts that will make you say, "I never looked at it that way," "I get it," or "That will work in my practice." *Profit from the Core* is titled perfectly for dentists. Many dentists want everything on the operational side of their practice to be as perfect as the dentistry they do. But seeking perfection with human beings is a misguided effort. However, seeking optimum performance in the core production drivers is not only smart, it's doable and highly profitable. And that, my friends, is exactly what I'm doing in this chapter: focusing on your biggest core driver: case acceptance to case scheduled to case completed.

Consistently growing production and collections by using the best decisions is far better than spurts of exceptional results marred by spurts of small disasters. Even worse, the small disasters usually aren't detected until the harm is done. Then, too many leaders in such predicaments try to drastically reverse their course, further exacerbating the problems. Wouldn't it be better if you knew how to prevent most of these disasters? The wealth of knowledge we have gleaned from a variety of leaders and a variety of industries can't be learned in a business school. We learned it by spending countless hours deep in the bowels of these organizations. By doing so, our clients are the beneficiaries.

Dentists are a special breed: smart and educated and forced to operate within a unique business model.

You have to be in production while you run your business!

You have to be *in* production while you *run* your business!

That's a unique, highly stressful, and very challenging situation. If you are sitting at your desk, mapping strategy and tactics, trying to optimize team performance and managing expenses, you are losing production. Conversely, if you are *in* production, when do you have time to strategize, implement, train, and measure improved practice performance? There are only so many hours in a day. When and how can a private-practice dentist create, implement, and manage effective systems to run the day-to-day operations of the practice? The better the systems and processes, the better the production and collections. Anything less than efficient and effective is costly, frustrating, and stressful.

Rome was not built in day. It was built based on one neighborhood at a time. So, don't assume that you need a process or procedure for every little thing your team does every day. It would be a huge waste of time and effort if you did. But your key production drivers, your focus, should be strategized and processed for maximum efficiency and effectiveness with due consideration for your patients, your team, and you. Leaving one of these stakeholders out of the equation is costly in many ways.

Strategy #4 will illuminate the significance of processes and systems as they relate to the gap between current production and the *next level* of production that, again, is easy to achieve with a well-thought-out process that fits your patients, your team, and you.

CASE ACCEPTANCE TO COMPLETION

As business strategists, our objective is to find the easiest and most meaningful production results for our clients as quickly as possible. Obviously, filling the schedule (doc and hygiene) is highly important. It's the front end of the economic engine of your practice. If you have zero open appointments, ostensibly, your practice will run at full speed. Right? Wrong! Why? Because, as you know, operatory production is *bigger* than hygiene production. Bigger is a relative word. How big is big? Look at it this way. You already know some patients with a treatment plan do not accept, schedule, and complete the treatment. Some of your patients simply can't afford the treatment. Many patients don't feel that they need the treatment at this time. They might say that the problem doesn't bother them right now, that they're too busy, or that they have other priorities or need to check with their spouse. In reality, they don't *want* to complete the treatment. They aren't motivated to complete the treatment. They don't understand the long-term consequences of not getting the treatment. They are procrastinators, and so on. The *value* isn't optimized. Interestingly, however, some of these patients will complete the treatment now.

We've measured this phenomenon in hundreds of practices. Here's the general rule: For every $100,000 of production a practice currently produces, another $20,000+ per month of production can rather easily be produced. Some of those patients who tend to procrastinate will want the treatment and will complete the treatment. For a $50,000-per-month practice, that's $10,000+ of new production per month. For a $200,000-per-month practice, that's $40,000 per month. It's an average increase of 20 percent in gross production, month-over-month.

How? You now know the magic key as MPSR: measurements, protocols, skills, and rewards.

Before I dive into some of the mechanics of MPSR related to case completion, I want to be clear that the 20 percent increase in new production is not related in any way to:

- getting more new patients;
- being more aggressive in your diagnosis; or
- pushing or selling dentistry in your practice.

It's really quite simple. It's about creating an environment in your practice so more patients will <u>want</u> the dentistry you diagnose. That's it!

—— CASE STUDY ——————————————————
Andalusia Dental Group

In the spring of 2012, I was the guest speaker for a Seattle Study Club chapter. Bill King, DMD, and Bob Burkhardt, DMD, are partners of Andalusia Dental Group, and they attended the event. In the ensuing weeks, our firm was engaged to help these dentists create a strategic plan for their practice. I delivered the plan on May 1 to Bill and Bob, and Bill's son, Parrish King, DMD, an associate. The practice was doing very well. According to my analysis and assessment, there were two key production drivers that could use a little tweaking, but only one KPD with a performance gap big enough to get serious: case acceptance to completion.

In June we began to redevelop the protocols for case completion with the doctors and the entire team. After several protocol drafts and editing, we launched the new protocol in early July with the doctors and team members and began the coaching phase for the communication skills to enhance the performance of the protocol. The objective for the rest of July was to get everyone comfortable with the new protocol and the skills. From their strategic plan, we already knew their measurement numbers for case completion. The only step needed in order to go live was the reward design for this KPD, which we finalized and communicated to the team.

On August 1 Andalusia Dental Group went live with the measurements, protocol, skills, and rewards to improve its case completion numbers. When the practice closed out the books for August, production had increased by 18 percent—in *one* month. After the launch of the case-acceptance-to-completion program at ADG, the practice maintained significant and sustainable new production, month over month. The practice's case completion numbers were above its baseline measurement every month as I wrote this book. That's sustainability! It happens when the MPSR system creates self-motivation in the team. The team members know the score, what to do, how to do it, and what they earn when the score is improved.

Similar results have been achieved again and again in hundreds of other practices. Not bad for a couple of strategic innovators who had no idea how the operational side of a dental practice worked until 2009.

Fred Jones and Phillip Vickery own a practice in a quaint town north of Nashville. Their story is similar to the story of Bill, Bob, and Parrish at Andalusia Dental Group. After developing a thorough strategic plan for Philip and Fred, it was evident that the practice was doing very well in most of their key production drivers. A few of their KPDs didn't have gaps to justify the time and expense of improvement compared to the potential production opportunity. However, their case completion results had plenty of room for improvement. In August 2013, we began the second step of MPSR: the protocol. We already knew their measurements. They were averaging 70 cases per month and the average production per case was $1,424. Common sense suggests that two or three more cases completed per week would be easy to achieve, and the new production of $14,000 to $20,000 per month would be well worth the effort. By example, I'll show you the how to.

—— CASE STUDY ——————————————————

Case Acceptance to Completion

Measurements:

Cases per month = 70

Production per case = $1,424

Protocol

In the fact-finding process of our strategic planning, we ask the dentist and a few team members about their protocol for case completion. For example, "I am a patient with a three o'clock prophy appointment today and the doctor will diagnose a crack in #3. What's the existing protocol from the time I enter the practice until I depart?"

Here's the typical answer I hear: "If the hygienist sees the crack, she will notify the dentist before he enters the operatory for the prophy check. The dentist will diagnose the crack in #3 and recommend a crown, and the hygienist will usher the patient to the front desk for a financial estimate and to schedule the appointment." That's it. Occasionally, I'll hear something about the hygienist discussing the problem and potential solutions, and maybe something about using models or an intraoral camera.

Now, go back to the original question: "What's the existing protocol from the time I <u>enter</u> the practice <u>until</u> I depart?" The question includes the phrase "from the time I enter the practice to the time I depart." But rarely does the answer include more than the basics. It's assumed that the primary patient engagements are with the hygienist, the doc, and the TX coordinator. With a significant production value, often exceeding $1,000, I would assert that acquiring the best protocol to optimize case completion is very important. But, in most practices, there is more angst over prophy patient no-shows and cancellations, and not attracting enough new patients. Yet prophy or new patient appointments do not average $1,000 in production. In fact, they're not even close. This is not to suggest that no-shows, cancellations, and a lack of new patients aren't important issues to be addressed. It *is* to suggest that the case completion protocol deserves priority attention for the benefit of your patients and the practice.

Your TX-plan patients have three big decisions to make:

1. To <u>accept</u> the treatment. Many patients accept TX, but do not schedule it.
2. To <u>schedule</u> the treatment. Many patients schedule TX, but either do not show or cancel.
3. To show up for their treatment appointment and <u>complete</u> the TX.

Assuming production and collections matter, doesn't it make sense to think through your case-acceptance-to-completion protocol to ensure it is comprehensive and accurate at every possible patient engagement?

Back to my protocol question. Answer the question as completely as possible, based on what you and your team do and say to a patient from entry to departure. Don't try to answer the question as you *want* the protocol to be, until you know how the protocol is followed *now*. Discuss the detail of team member and doctor engagements at every touch point that the patient experiences, from greeting to goodbye. Next, convert your notes to a written document. That's your existing protocol. Now you can discuss the protocol as you think it *should* be. The real question then becomes, "How can we find the absolute best protocol for our practice?" At $1,000+/- per case, you really want to get this protocol as perfect as you can, because you only get one best chance at acceptance, scheduling, and completion. So, getting it right for you and your team may be different from what you think you need. Don't cut corners on your case completion protocol! It's worth finding the best protocol.

Skills

So far, we know the measurements and we know what to do (the protocol) to improve the measurements. Next step? We need to know *how* (the skills) to do the *what* in order to best deliver the protocol. Would you agree that what we say and how we say it matters? Communication skills have a profound effect on the level of success you and your team experience in case acceptance, scheduling, and completion, along with every other key production driver. How about the level of professionalism being demonstrated? Professionalism matters because how the patient feels about the overall experience affects the patient's decision to accept, schedule, and complete the treatment.

This will be a short section of this chapter, because I don't need to duplicate the communication skills that have already been discussed. Regardless of where you and your team live and work, or what kind of personal backgrounds and education you have, there are basic communication skills and professionalism that make a difference in how you serve your patients and prospective patients. I'm reminded of comments I've heard. "But John, we are in a small town in southwest Kansas and we don't talk like they do in Kansas City." Or "I'm not going to memorize scripts." I couldn't agree more! Just make sure you and your team own and use the basics, the fundamentals. Communication skills have to be used by a team member in a manner most comfortable for that team member but also in a manner that serves the purpose of increasing a patient's desire to complete the diagnosed dentistry. When the best communication skills are not used, the patient is less likely to complete the TX, which defeats the purpose. Here's the main point: consistency of communication among you and your team is very important.

As consumers and patients, we do not like to hear or experience inconsistencies in communication. In a dental practice, inconsistencies in communications will occur if there is no effective effort to prevent them. What we say and how we say it matters, more than you might realize. You already have read the chapter on the patient experience. In this chapter, we are discussing case completion. Communication skills affect the patient experience and your results, from the acceptance of more treatments to scheduling the TX and completing the TX.

Rewards

Before we cover this last piece of the MPSR formula to improve case completion, please do not assume that the reward is the most important piece, that it trumps the protocol and skills in any way. That would be a costly mistake. Tens of thousands of dental practices have some form of bonus or incentive plan. In today's economy most of them are ineffective in motivating the team. The payouts are sporadic (further demotivating the team), and the return on investment to the owner is much less than desirable (further diminishing the owner's motivation to provide some form of reward).

To accomplish the objective of improving these $1,000+/- production opportunities that are available every day in almost every practice, let's create some form of incentive that motivates the dentist/owner and motivates the team to perform the protocol and execute the skills needed to improve case acceptance to completion.

In Philip and Fred's case, they and their team members now know their baseline measurement, the protocol, and the skills. So, everyone knows the score, knows what to do to improve the score, and knows how to improve the score. The reward, designed the right way, is the *ribbon and the bow* on their new gift: improved case completion. You have always wanted your team members to perform to their capabilities, not just work harder or work smarter. Preferably, you really want your team to follow a specific protocol that serves your patients better and rewards the team and you very well.

The reward is, obviously, designed to improve your case completion baseline score. But that happens when the best-designed protocol is followed and the best skills are used. Like Philip and Fred's baseline score of 70, you want that number to increase to, say, 80, 90, 100, or 110. What's realistic? Well, as I sit here, pecking away at my laptop, I'm looking at Philip and Fred's last three months of results of 106, 108, and 96. That's 36, 38, and 26 more cases than the original baseline average of 70 per month. At $1,424 per case, you can do the math for each month and total the new production. Got it?

Here are a few more examples of practices living the dream of taking case acceptance to completion.

1. Solo GP: Original baseline score = 28. New average score = 47. That is 19 more x $1,156 = $21,964 additional average production per month.

2. Two GP doctors: Original baseline score = 74. New average score = 103. That is 29 more x $979 = $28,391 additional average production per month.

3. Three doctors: Original score = 107. New average score = 156. That is 49 more x $1,384 = $ 67,816 additional average production per month.

Clearly, you see the major improvement in the number of cases and the corresponding improvement in production. How long does it usually take to hit a peak level of cases completed? In most situations the first month of tracking results will show a small improvement in the number of cases completed. More importantly, you will experience your team members following the protocol. They bought in! As the leader, make sure that the protocol is followed and maintain the focus on it.

The second month (as the protocols and skills are delivered better and more naturally), your case completion number should make a respectable upward movement and now you know the first month wasn't a fluke. By the end of month three, your new case completion strategy is becoming a habit and has positively affected production, collections, and profit. Your team is earning an incentive and they understand they have much of the control over the results—by following the protocol and using the skills.

In the long term, expect the monthly case completion number to reach a pinnacle and to fluctuate to some extent, month over month, such as 30 more in a month, then 32 more, 26 more, 27 more, 36 more. Rarely will you experience big ups and downs, because the team gets it. But vacations and holidays can, and will, negatively affect capabilities simply because doc workdays are lower than average. Once you are up and running and past the fourth or fifth month of tracking, you will rarely see big movements. On the other hand, capacity to improve can become an issue when your doc open appointments are consistently in the single digits, month over month. That's a great problem to have! Then, it's time to add another operatory, find more space, and so on. When you are scheduling TX patients two months in advance, it's time to think about a different issue. Perhaps it's time to find an associate. It's a lot of fun to be a part of solving a capacity problem because the dentist and team have maximized a core component of the business.

Back to the incentive designed specifically for case completion: First, you'll need to know your average case completion score per month, which means you'll have to define a case. We have tried and tested numerous definitions. Over the years, we've determined there are specific qualifiers to define a case. Here they are:

1. The definition has to be easy to understand by all team members.
2. It has to be easy to measure by the dentist and team members.
3. It has to be easy to track at any time.
4. It has to be doc production only, not hygiene.
5. It has to entail a relevant amount of production.
6. It can't be focused on big cases.

About #6: Yes, you want big cases, but they are few and far between, and you can't pay the bills and make a profit with just big cases. So, get all of the big cases you can. But those $500, $1,800, and $3,300 cases are being diagnosed all day long. Why not use the best protocols and best skills all day every day to help as many patients as possible acquire the dentistry you have diagnosed? When 15 or 25 or 50 more patients accept, schedule, and complete the TX per month, at an average of anywhere from $900 per case to $2,500 per case, you'll be very pleased, as will your team and your patients.

In #5 above, I mentioned relevant production. The objective is to find a minimum production value for a measurement. This has nothing to do with patients' ability to pay, or how much effort will be expended by you and your team to help patients get the dentistry they need. The point is to eliminate very small cases, since the vast majority of these will be completed anyway…single fillings, sealants, etc.

Find Your Baseline

Print three months of doc production day sheets. Decide on your minimum *production per patient per day*. We typically use $350 to $500 for small-town PPO practices and big-city, high-end cosmetic practices. Don't fret over this number. Pick a production value and move on. Count the number of patients per day that have $350 (or $500) of doc-only production (regardless of the procedures). It's not about the number of TX plans (that's too hard to track). It's about production per patient per day, using your minimum number as your baseline. Use three months of data to achieve a reasonable average per month. Do not get into the game of trying to track how many were accepted or scheduled. All you want to know is how many cases were *completed*.

Find Your Average Production per Case

Let's say you chose to use $350 as your minimum case. Then, what's your average production per case? Simple. Add the production for all of the cases noted above and divide it by the total number of cases, and you'll know your average production per case. This will include every case from your minimum production value to the biggest case for all three months. The case studies discussed in this book used $350 or $500 as the minimum. From Maine to Florida, from Cincinnati to Philadelphia to Atlanta, and in many small towns, I've personally done the scoring noted above. Using $350 as the minimum production, I've seen average production per case range from $787 to $2,531. All you want is a realistic measurement per case. The exercise I just described can take an hour or more. Once it's done, it's done. Moving forward you'll be tracking these numbers daily, and that can be accomplished in seconds.

To build out your incentive plan, you'll want to create multiple levels for your team with the first level at an easy-to-achieve increase from the baseline. The second and subsequent levels will use the same improvement number for the first level. Each full-time team member should receive $100 per month for the first level, $200 per month for the second level, and so on. Part-timers should earn a prorated payout based on days or hours worked.

What about you and your practice? First, let's do a little before-and-after comparison. If you have, or have had, a production-based bonus program, or a combination of a production-based and a collections-based bonus program (or, maybe, it has even included a factor for payroll expense or profitability), here's what's generally happening:

1. Your team members, typically, have no idea how the bonus is calculated. That's a problem. If they don't understand it, how can they perform to achieve it?

2. Even if they have an idea how it's calculated, they don't connect the dots from what they do all day to how it affects the calculation. If, by chance, the practice is on track to hit the monthly goal by mid-month, some of the team members start to scramble to find production. Not good! Patients feel the push!

3. During the few months when a payout is actually earned, 20 percent of the overage goes to the team (to split) and

80 percent goes to the dentist. The percentage might seem favorable to you, but if you aren't hitting the goal, it doesn't matter. No one wins. By the way, your CPA will tell you that should the goal be achieved, your share of the pot is a 4:1 return on investment.

4. The team gets discouraged when the goal is achieved a few times and, subsequently, the goal is raised. They are back to "It's a job. I'll do my work and go home."

5. Bottom line: This type of bonus is rarely effective.

Re-think!

1. Wouldn't you rather have an incentive reward specifically designed to improve performance and production in a specific key production driver your team is engaged in every day?

2. Wouldn't your team members perform better and more consistently if they had a defined protocol to help them be the best that they can be?

3. Wouldn't your team members be more motivated if they knew the score for what you want them to improve, and if they had the protocol to guide them and the skills to achieve a goal with multiple levels of rewards?

4. Wouldn't your team members perform better month over month when they have earned an incentive every month, with very few exceptions? Consistency matters.

Now, What's in It for You?

1. First, scrap the old 4:1 return on investment. How about a 10:1 ROI? That's much better…250 percent better for you and your team wins, too.

2. You and your team know exactly what to do and how to do it to achieve an easy-to-understand goal that has multiple levels.

3. Everybody knows the score every day and can know the score any time during the day, which is customary. Self-motivated focus is amazing!

4. You see and experience a level of performance you have never seen before, because your team knows what to do and how to do it and is rewarded for doing it. So are you—at a 10:1 ROI.

5. Incentives are earned virtually every month because team members have the control and ability to make it happen. Therefore, they repeat and repeat and repeat. That's sustainability.

6. Your production, collections, and profit achieve levels that were only dreams and wishes a few months ago.

I remember (how could I forget?) the day I determined how to measure the baseline number for case completion. A few days later, we had a sample protocol for the practice. We already had the skills part but made a few adjustments to align with the sample protocol. The incentive design was a knock-off of one of the designs we used for a few of our community bank clients. Within two weeks I was back at the same practice, where the measurements were unearthed. It took the doctor a few minutes to understand the mechanics and the psychology. We initiated the measurements, protocols, skills, and rewards. The doctor's baseline was 28. In the first month the team hit 37, the next month 45, and they topped out at 52. It's been in the 50+/- range ever since—for 3.5 years. That's 34 more cases per month, and production improved from $85,000+/- to more than $115,000 per month. We frequently look back on that watershed time. To us it was like discovering a new drug to cure a killer disease. We had cracked the code. We had found the formula that creates team performance, sustainably.

Case Acceptance to Completion: Innovate or Stagnate or Wither!

At Dental Team Performance we help dentist/owners improve taking case acceptance to scheduling to completion. It's the number-one production driver for every practice we've had the pleasure of serving. In many ways, the strategy and tactics that improve case completion numbers also serve to minimize the day-to-day frustrations of dentists and team members. Why? Because everybody knows what to do and how to do it. Self-motivation becomes the rule of the day rather than mediocrity. Fun and success returns, and team performance invades the practice. Your patients win, your team members win, and you win! Discover how you can improve taking case acceptance to completion in your practice by visiting www.whydtp.com or calling 800-943-9638.

CHAPTER FIVE

LEADERSHIP TO TEAM PERFORMANCE

STRATEGY #5

Leading is often confused with managing. We manage our investments, our budget, and our time. In other words, we manage *things*. But should we manage people or lead them? Let's look at each style for a moment.

Managing people is synonymous with telling them to do this or that, or to not do this or that. The great business leaders and scholars refer to managing people as a *push strategy*. To make my point, when you tell your child to stop throwing rocks, your child's natural response is to stop throwing rocks temporarily, until you are gone, at which time the rock throwing continues. Now, flip the example to you, personally. Even as an adult, do *you* like to be told what to do, when to do it, and how to do it? Probably not. Do you think your team members like to be told what to do? Most likely not. When managing and telling are the primary behaviors and tools used to get things accomplished in a dental practice, rest assured, practice production falls far short of its full potential. Why? Someone has to do the work around here, right? Yep! But, a manager typically views the work, the to-do list, as very important. The work needs to get completed, but the work list very likely will not include a laser focus on your key production drivers. If your KPDs aren't the main focus, absent sheer luck, you can't achieve accelerated team performance and, therefore, production will not approach your reasonable expectations.

If you have job descriptions, take a look at them. Do the job descriptions specifically address performing to impact your key production drivers? Probably not! Most likely, the job descriptions are about getting work done, the to-do list.

In this book you've read many examples of misdirected work that does not maximize production. As a refresher, assume I'm a dentist for a moment. My doc and hygiene schedules consistently have too many open appointments. With little forethought, I have decided to solve the problem by updating my website, creating a Facebook page, and starting a direct mail program, all for the purpose of attracting more new patients. The costs? A bunch! The results? A gamble! The return on investment? Low to negative! Conversely, I could have evaluated why our schedule is so open. Had I evaluated the *why*, I would have found that my practice has served 2,876 active patients in the last 18 months; our referral-to-new-patient ratio is 16 percent; our recall efforts have no protocol, not the best skills, and no objective accountability; and we do very little to minimize no-shows and cancellations. I would have learned much more than that, but those indicators would tell me my new patient target is not the best use of our time, talent, and money. I'm aiming at the wrong target. I would ask myself why we need more new patients when we already have nearly 3,000 patients who know, like, and trust us? Why not improve our internal operations and focus on the best solutions to fill the schedule with existing patients? Had I created the measurements, protocols, skills, and rewards to reduce no-shows and cancellations and increase referrals and recall results, my open appointments would have, predictably, been reduced. I would have saved our team members lots of time and frustration, and saved myself lots of money. Mission accomplished! More of our active patients would have been served with the dentistry they needed and wanted. As a result, our production would have improved, predictably and significantly. Working harder and working smarter are admirable. But why complicate it, when you and your team can perform with a key focus that achieves the best results and do it efficiently and effectively?

Leadership is the opposite of managing. If managing is pushing, then leading is pulling. Leadership is about creating a practice environment that engages team members to *want* to perform, not just work hard and not just get things done. Performance connotes results, the intended results of the leader. In the most successful organizations, focused performance *is* the culture. If a dental practice does not have a well-thought-out and defined short list of key performance strategies, then it's impossible to perform well. It is impossible to perform, based on what is unknown or unclear. In other words, the expectations are not absolutely clear. I've seen this many times, in nonprofits and for-profits, in big and small organizations, and in multiple industries. Thousands of books have been written on the subject of leading based on expectations, several of which were mentioned in Chapter Four.

Leadership is the genesis of successful organizations. Are leaders born or can people learn to be leaders? No doubt, some people have natural leadership tendencies. But, more often, leadership is learned. Private-practice dentist/owners are like the rest of us business owners. We are trying to lead our team members to efficiently and effectively help us grow our businesses. That's it! Unfortunately, few of us are skilled leaders when we open the doors to do business with our prospective customers. Worse yet, without the core competencies of leadership, we biz owners have a tendency to morph more frequently down the path of management. That said, I've seen many biz owners responsible for team performance graduate from being ineffective managers to becoming good leaders. And, I might add, leadership applies to office managers, as well. Just change the title of the position to office administrator, or some other applicable name. Eliminate any reference to *manage, managing,* or *management.*

Thus far, I hope I've made two big points:

1. Be a leader, not a manager
2. Lead *to* your key performance focus

I'll use #2 above to frame the essence of leadership. And, since I've discussed several key production drivers in previous chapters, my hope is to give you a common-sense formula you can use immediately.

Key Production Drivers

- Patient Experience to Profit (Chapter One)
- Fill the Schedule to Production (Chapter Three)
- Case Acceptance to Completion (Chapter Four)

Leading any of these three KPDs above, or all three, will serve you, your team, and your patients very well. Here's the step-by-step methodology.

Leadership to Team Performance

To upgrade your leadership skills, you can go to Amazon.com and search for books with *leadership* in the title. You'll find over 250,000+ books on the subject of leadership. Buy a few books and learn how to be a leader, or get the "CliffNotes" in this chapter, specifically for dental practices.

Four Steps

1. **Set clear expectations.** How? Remember MPSR specific to any of your key production drivers:

   □ Measurements: know the score in the KPD to set clear objective expectations.

   □ Protocols: with your team, develop the *what to do* for clear expectations.

   □ Skills: provide the best communication skills to ensure that the protocol can be followed to improve the chance of achieving the objective.

   □ Rewards: establish easy-to-understand rewards for achieving the expected outcome.

Now, that's not so hard, is it?

2. **Communicate clear expectations.**

   □ From #1, put the protocols in writing: for each KPD, ensure that everyone clearly understands the *why, what, when, how* and *who,* to optimize performance. This also creates a high degree of accountability with the team and the doctor.

   □ Verbally: include communicating the protocol in team meetings and huddles.

   □ Don't assume everyone has a photographic memory. Repetition of the protocols keeps expectations front and center.

3. **Evaluate performance based on expectations.**

   □ Objective evaluations are best: team performance can be measured, objectively, based on your baseline KPD score and achieving the improved measurement levels.

◻ Subjective evaluations work too, assuming you have written protocols for the focused KPD and the ability to visually or verbally evaluate performance. It's unlikely that you can subjectively evaluate all of the steps in a specific protocol, but it is rather easy to evaluate parts of the protocol subjectively.

◻ Objective and subjective evaluations can be used in team meetings and morning huddles.

4. **Continuously improve performance.**

◻ MPSR is a powerful resource. It serves hundreds of dentists with multiple benefits, including creating a team of happy performers, a significant increase in production, less stress and frustration, and a deep of sense of relief that the practice is on a solid operational foundation. It improves team members' ability to meet the dentist's expectations, creates a true team spirit, improved operational efficiencies, and rewards team members very well. Wow! Sign me up! Can this actually happen? Yes, but to different degrees. How do you honestly feel about the current state of affairs in your practice? Regardless of how you rate your practice, applying MPSR to one or more of the key production drivers will make a big difference, as has been noted. Perfection, however, is neither a goal nor a possibility. But continuously improving your leadership skills *is* the goal, because leadership is the foundation of the success of your team and, thus, your practice.

◻ When a leader-dentist implements the strategies of this book, good things happen, and they can happen quickly. Therefore, continuous improvements in a dental practice begins with a leadership mindset instead of a management mindset. Like any other performance measure, continuous improvements deliver better results. As the leader leads, so the team performs.

▫ When the protocols are developed, they are never perfect. Your team, patients, and operations are constantly in movement. Based on our experiences over many years, we recommend that our clients do not continually update their protocols for every minor issue. Micromanaging the protocol is a big mistake. Team members will lose interest in performing, which defeats the purpose. Not good! But updates will be needed. Frankly, it's best to update or upgrade your protocols no more often than every six months. Exceptions can happen. If a major situation arises that warrants a protocol update, do it.

Continuous improvements are best created by continuously focusing on following the protocols as designed and agreed upon by doctor and team members, and improving the communication skills that support the specific KPD protocol. Nothing else will improve results better!

- Continuous improvements are best created by continuously focusing on *following the protocols as designed and agreed upon by doctor and team members*, and improving the communication skills that support the specific KPD protocol. Nothing else will improve results better!

- For those who deny the leadership mission and stick with a managing mindset, improving team performance and the results of the practice will be a continuing struggle. Remember you can manage things, but to improve team performance to production, collections, and profit, leadership is the key.

Office Administrators

Office administrators can be a dream come true for a dentist/owner. But they have to be aligned with the leader-dentist, leading MPSR on behalf of the dentist. As a popular TV commercial notes, "It isn't complicated." As another popular TV commercial states, "Just do it." A key word here is *aligned*. Too often, office administrators have little or no experience managing or leading people. The position was created to deflect daily issues from the dentist/owner, such as directing patient flow, dealing with personnel issues and maintaining adequate staffing. Show me a practice with a dentist leader and an office administrator leader and I'll show you a practice with very few personnel issues. Plus, production, collections, and profit will improve.

Earlier I briefly mentioned the *Policies and Procedures* manual. It's a very important part of your practice. But I recommend that, as a leader, you keep the *Performance Protocols* separate from the *Policies and Procedures* manual, both mentally and physically. The two do not fit together. To team members, each has a totally different connotation. Policies and procedures are necessary, but keep in mind it's all about the to-do list: the work. Conversely, your performance protocols are about performing based on your key production drivers that affect production. Don't connect work with performance!

Leadership is a major missing link for most business owners. Any business owner can initiate leadership skills at any time without the M, P, S, or R. The question is what will the end result be? Is it measurable? Does it make a meaningful difference? Leadership to team performance is specific, results based, and founded on human nature, facts, and processes. The results are measurable, significant, and sustainable for you, your team members, and your patients. Think about it!

—— CASE STUDY ——

Dr. Amy Hartsfield and Team

Dr. Amy is a perfect example of a dentist who graduated from *managing* to *leading*. With her strategic plan and key production drivers implemented, Amy could see her team members' performance improvements, as well as a few performance flaws that needed more attention. While the planned and predictable production growth was happening, it became obvious that being a full-time producing dentist and leading a successful business required delegation. Soon, Amy appointed Stacey as office manager. Dr. Amy aligned Stacey with their strategic plan, including the key production drivers of the practice, to maintain the focus on team performance. Stacey earned the authority to lead the team. The two have become a dynamic duo, leading the practice to exceptional levels of production and collections. In the last two years, Amy's practice has grown by 16.77 percent.

While team members' performance has a profound impact on production and collections, leadership of team performance sets the expectations for the team with objective accountability.

While team members' performance has a profound impact on production and collections, leadership of team performance sets the expectations for the team with objective accountability.

At Dental Team Performance, we help dentist/owners become leaders with a defined focus specific to the needs of their practice. Leadership is the bond that makes everything else perform to its potential, clinically and operationally. Your patients win, your team members win and you win! Discover how you can be a leader-dentist by visiting www.whydtp.com or calling 800-943-9638.

CHAPTER SIX

EXECUTING YOUR PLAN

GREAT INFORMATION, NO EXECUTION, WASTED LIFE CHANGER

All hat and no cows! That's what they say in Texas when someone talks-the-talk but doesn't walk-the-walk. Business owners, dentists included, can learn every best practice strategy and tactic, but without a decision to move forward and execute the strategy or tactic, it's just knowledge. There is no shortage of information to help you grow your practice. You can attend boot camps, seminars, and continuing education lectures, or buy a truck load of CDs and DVDs and Google until your fingers bleed. But, as Kevin O'Leary says on the TV show *Shark Tank*, "Stop the insanity!"

At some point, assuming you want to grow your practice, you'll have to decide how to use the information and knowledge you have learned to achieve your goals. Maybe you have a better fail-safe method. I'm sticking with creating a strategic plan to succeed. Assuming you have developed your overarching strategy with the best tactics for your practice, how you implement the strategy will dictate your results. "But John, where do I start?" Go back to Chapter Two. Get a strategic plan! It's common sense. Know before you go! Don't grab an idea such as "improve recall," "get more new patients," or "start a periodontal program" unless your strategic plan tells you that it is a key production driver for your practice. It should tell you the gap opportunity, the financial opportunity, and how to close the gap. With your strategic plan, you have all of the quantifiable evidence you to need to make an intelligent decision based on the facts. It's time to go!

Now, it's time to implement or execute your plan. You've made a decision to go. May I suggest that the first step in execution is really a pre-step. Here's why. Have you ever heard a really great idea at a continuing education lecture, implemented the idea the following week with your team, and waited anxiously for the promised improvement? I have done this, and I know plenty of dentists who have done the same. But the results I expected didn't happen. "Well, darn it," you say. "That didn't work. The presenter at the continuing education lecture—or the promised benefits on the DVD—was just smoke and mirrors. I'll never listen to him again." Gun shy, you wait a long time before trying again.

People buy in and commit to what they help create.

The problem usually isn't the quality of the information delivered by the presenter or the info in the DVD; it's misguided implementation. Even with a comprehensive strategic plan developed and communicated verbally and in writing with the dentist, the implementation can be a dud if the execution process isn't well thought out before introducing it to the team members. In fact, a properly crafted strategic plan includes the team members at the beginning of the fact finding, and throughout the process. And that's the pre-step: involving your team members in the planning on the front end. People buy-in and commit to what they help create. Their potential fears and objections can be resolved before they become fears and objections.

When a few team members are excited and engaged in the process and engaged in solving problems and strategizing for the prospective improvement, others follow. Peer pressure beats dentist pressure. Team performance is starting to brew. Plus, team members' input can be invaluable, as often they know more about a problem than the dentist. Makes sense, doesn't it? Now, you may be thinking, this takes way too much time and effort. Frankly, it saves time and effort, because a few hours invested in the pre-step will greatly enhance the level of success in the execution of your plan and the intended results. The two main objectives of the pre-step are to fend off negativity before it starts and create as much team buy-in before you execute anything.

Think about that. Would you trade a few hours of pre-step effort for an additional $10,000 or $15,000 or $40,000 per month in new and sustainable production? I would hope so! And that's what you want: the results you should achieve and all of the benefits, including more production and less stress and frustration. One would think most of us would be quite pleased with such a return on investment.

In Chapter Two, I shared the process to develop a strategic plan. We call it Strategic Planning to Focus, because by comprehensively analyzing and evaluating your practice, you can effectively define your *focus*. By doing so, two very important things happen: 1) you can eliminate work efforts that have been assumed to be important or effective but aren't, and 2) your improved strategic focus allows your team and you to invest your valuable time and efforts on what has the biggest impact on your practice. That's critically important, because time is a valuable commodity in most practices. As the leader, you do not want to gamble your time, efforts, and reputation with your team on a prospective strategy that doesn't serve your patients and your team members better and improve production and collections. If all three parties win, your planned strategy and tactics earn the right to be executed.

Regardless of your current production level, you want your practice to be efficient and effective. You want to have the right people in the right positions in your practice. You want these right team members to be as effective as possible to best serve your patients. You want your team members to be as efficient as possible in their positions to optimize your payroll expense and their performance. Am I right, so far?

Developing your strategic plan is a must to help you invest your time, effort, and money with the biggest bang for the buck. But the end goal isn't just about production or money. We have served plenty of dentists whose primary goal has nothing to do with production. Clearly, their primary goal was fixing the inefficiencies, including having our help with making the patient-flow make sense for the patients and team; making the hygiene and operatory scheduling synchronize; or finding the best way to verify, file, and collect insurance benefits. Developing your strategic plan will essentially put all of the cards on the table so you can see them all. Then, the key production drivers and inefficiencies can be evaluated, based on the facts so you can decide on the things that matter most to you, operationally and economically. Execution follows.

EXECUTING YOUR KEY PRODUCTION DRIVERS

A Strategic Plan to Focus is highly important for all of the reasons noted in this book. With a plan, typically, three to five KPDs will be determined, the ones that matter most for the practice. That's the focus. Let's say your strategic plan includes four KPDs: patient experience, filling the schedule, case completion, and leadership. Now, how do you execute all four? Answer: it depends. But first, do not try to execute all four at the same time! It's too much, too fast for you and your team. If *production* is your priority goal, then case completion is the first KPD to execute, for several reasons: 1) it offers the biggest production opportunity, 2) it's the easiest KPD you and your team can improve, and 3) it's the fastest KPD to improve. Plus, the sooner you and your team experience results in your strategic plan, the sooner everyone's confidence in the entire plan can be realized. Case completion is the ticket to an early confidence builder for your team, which enhances team buy-in for the next KPD.

To execute case acceptance to completion, review Chapter Four. From a time perspective, you probably want it completed, executed yesterday. Think about the story of *Goldilocks and the Three Bears*: not too hot and not too cold, but just right. Case completion should also be *not too fast and not too slow but just right*. From the kick-off meeting for the patient-flow protocol to launching the protocol and incentive plan, 30 to 60 days is a reasonable window of time.

What's your next KPD to execute? Again, it depends. If open appointments are a problem, the fill-the-schedule KPD would be appropriate. Go to Chapter Three for the execution detail. In this KPD, you can pick and choose among the multiple tactics. Each one has a purpose. Do not discount any of them. Together they will minimize open appointments.

The patience experience is detailed in Chapter One. Follow the yellow brick road as noted, and you will be able to quantifiably measure improvements in your telephone mystery call scores and your in-office patient experience scores. These two objective measurements provide you with the objective accountability to improve the score, and to recognize and reward your team for the improvements.

Executing leadership to team performance is rather easy. In the big picture, it can be plugged in anywhere in the overall strategic plan execution process. Our experience suggests initiating leadership after the first KPD has been fully implemented works best because at that point, the dentist has a complete set of measurements, protocols, skills, and rewards in place and in action. With these, all of the pieces of the puzzle are in place for you to be a leader-dentist. You can set clear expectations, communicate clear expectations, evaluate clear expectations, and continuously improve clear expectations.

For example, leading your case completion strategy is quite easy. Everyone knows the baseline score and how it is measured. All your team members know the protocol, because they helped create it and it's in writing. They all know the patient-engagement communications skills and clearly understand the reward when the case completion baseline score is improved. There should be no doubts. Let's say your case completion strategy includes a baseline measurement of 38 cases per month. I'll assume that your first level of incentives is at 45, the second level is at 52, and the third level is at 59. If each new case is worth $1,000 in new production, then each level is worth $7,000 per month in new production. Are you interested in your team achieving the first level, the second level, and even the third level? I'm guessing you are very interested. At the second level, everyone is wondering why this couldn't have been done in the past. At the third level, everyone is dumbfounded by the results. There isn't a thought about working harder. Self-motivation and performance is in full bloom. And yes, $21,000+/- of new production is on the monthly production report. Amazing, right? In a way, I agree it is amazing. What happened to your practice? You've found your focus in your key production drivers. You've found the best protocol to improve the score in each KPD. Communication skills? Improved! Rewards, both recognition and financial, fan the flame of results, consistently. Congratulations! Step by step, you were a leader of the process.

Leaders are cheerleaders. Leaders are encouragers. Leaders know the fundamentals (the protocols), and they keep their teams focused on the fundamentals. Leaders keep score. You should post the daily score in the break room, adding the number of cases needed to achieve the next level, and the next level. Leaders pay attention to the objective and subjective sides of accountability. If using intraoral cameras is a part of your protocol, it is very easy to ensure that your team members understand why, what, how, and when. See? This isn't hard and the benefits are significant and sustainable.

Now, here's the best part. I've experienced this phenomenon with many practices. I was helping a dentist launch his case completion strategy and leadership via telecoaching. He asked me to jointly work through the protocol part with his team. Within a few minutes after the team/doc teleconference ended, the dentist called me back and said, "John, my team left our teleconference meeting with total excitement about being a part of improving our case completion results." I said, "They are supposed to be excited." He said, "I know you told me that, but I didn't believe it. I've never seen them excited about anything in this practice except when I implemented paid time off." Fast-forward 60 days or so. His team hit the second level of tracking the score, and each team member received $200. The phone rang again. It was the doc. "John, this is incredible," he said. Playing dumb, I asked him to explain what was so incredible. He said, "They want to know what happens when they hit the third level. Can they add another level?" Calmly, I asked him what he wanted to do. He said, "Are your kidding? I add $8,000 in new production at each level. Damn right I want to add another level." So, I said, "Doc, it's your practice. Add another level if you so desire." I did ask him to explain what was motivating his team members to perform so well. He said, "They just *feel* everyone is on the same page for the first time in a long time. They *feel* good about how we are all serving our patient's needs by following the protocol and coming to work is fun." Admittedly, similar stories are common.

The execution of your key production drivers starts with the development of your protocols and ends with the improvement of the measurement. Think of it as you might think of a sport—soccer, for example. My youngest son played on an Olympic development team. Practice, practice, practice! On many occasions a few of the parents would hang around during practice. I heard the coach yell, "Finish" many, many times. He would say, "Boys, we can run up and down the field all day long, but if we do not score, it doesn't matter." So, look at execution as practicing to finish. You are the coach, the leader. Get your MPSR created, launched and executed, and finish—score.

At Dental Team Performance, executing a strategic plan and the key production drivers, including developing leadership to impact team performance, is how we help dentist/owners succeed beyond their thoughts and dreams. Executing your plan is the grand finale—the way to finish, to make the plan pay off for your patients, team members, and you. Discover how you can execute your strategic plan and your key production drivers by calling us at 800-943-9638.

CHAPTER SEVEN

RETAINING YOUR NEW RESULTS

YOU ACHIEVED IT! DON'T LOSE IT!

The foundational pieces of your next level of success have been duly noted in prior chapters:

- focus
- key production drivers
- MPSR
- leadership
- execution

Let's assume you are average at all five of these foundational pieces. If so, you'll increase production from 15 percent to 20 percent. For an $800,000 practice, that's $120,000 to $160,000 more of new production per year. You and your team members will be very pleased and the MPSR will be second nature. Imagine your personal financial health, the financial health of your practice, and the rewards of incentives and recognition for your team by plugging along with an average performance in your strategic plan for three, five, or ten years. A $150,000 increase in annual production for five years adds $750,000 to the production coffers of your practice. I'm not suggesting that average performance with your strategic plan is your goal, but I am suggesting that exceptional performance is not required to experience a significant improvement in production, collections, and profit.

Above-average practice performers routinely achieve a 25 percent increase in production. Leader-dentists and team members subscribing to a continuous-improvement mindset achieve a high level of performance. Often, this group achieves a 30 to 45 percent improvement in production over three or more years from the original baseline production. That's with little or no increase in personnel.

Whether average, above average, or excellent, the one thing that each of these dentists will say is it's team performance that impacts the key production drivers that achieves the results.

> *Whether average, above average, or excellent, the one thing that each of these dentists will say is it's team performance that impacts the key production drivers that achieves the results.*

And it's the truth! I know I have pounded this team performance concept throughout this book. That's intentional, because for some reason, so many dentists just don't believe team performance can accomplish these amazing results, year over year. I've heard, "What's the gimmick?" "What's the hidden secret?" "There's no way my team can do this." "I'll have to fire every employee and start all over." "This will not work in my market." "You don't understand our patient mix," and many more excuses. I've heard them all, but I've also been helping businesses optimize team performance to impact production for 27 years, so excuses are lame, lazy and irrelevant.

But there are no guarantees! Making assumptions is not a good business trait. It will take five to eight months to get all of your KPDs launched and your new economic engine up to a 20 percent increase in production, month over month. Then, it's embedded in your team and you, and life is good. What could possibly undermine these results? I can think of five performance killers you want to avoid.

1. Complacency Can and Will Kill Team Performance!

You and your team have created your strategic plan with KPDs and MPSR, and you are off to the races. Production is up significantly and you are leading your team. The doubts about this not working have vanished. Caution. Think of your new performance as a balloon. You and your team have blown air into the balloon to inflate it. However, your balloon has a few pinholes in it, representing anything that can negatively affect the focus on the protocols and skills. It happens, so don't assume it can't or won't, because it can and will. Knowing this up front will help you see it and deal with it, and more importantly, prevent it. A few daily or weekly puffs of protocol air, skills air, and leadership air will keep the complacency wolves away.

Complacency will erode the results in short order. All you have to do is take your eye off of the ball. Don't! Remember what you did to get to the optimum production level in your practice? Remember what you did to lead your team? Get complacent (you and your team members) and production will gradually diminish. By the time you realize what is happening, you've lost some serious production that is not retrievable anytime soon. You have lost momentum and it can take several months to get it back. Now, assuming you want to get back to the good times, you have to reignite yourself and your team. Clearly, you know what to do, because you've done it before. Get back on track with your MPSR in your KPDs. Frankly, complacency in following the *protocols* is usually the culprit. I beg of you to keep the <u>protocols</u> alive and well *every day*, *every week* and *every month*.

2. Pay the Incentives—on Time

When incentives are earned, pay your team as soon as possible and be happy about it. Your ROI is likely to be in the 10:1 range, so it's not a matter of having it to pay it.

3. Messing with the Incentive Design

Do not increase the baseline score or adjust the incentive levels. A deal with your team is a deal. If you do play games with the incentive, you might squeeze a few bucks out of what you otherwise would have paid your team, but you would also lose the trust of your team and the game will be compromised or be over.

4. On-Board New Team Members, Quickly

Team member turnover should be minimal once your strategic plan is operational. However, for legitimate reasons over time, team members do leave. When a new team member joins your practice, what's your on-boarding process to acclimate the newbie to your practice? If you do not have an on-boarding process, may I suggest a few thoughts:

- Before you make an offer to a potential new team member, ask the candidate to read your strategic plan <u>protocols</u> (only). Tell him or her, "This is the way our practice *performs*. I will need to know that you understand these protocols before we discuss next steps."
- During your new hire's first few days, make sure the newbie understands the M, the P, the S, and the R for each key production driver. Enlist your other team members to

help the newbie clearly understand and use the protocols as expected.

- Doc: evaluate the newbie early and often to ensure she gets it, uses it, and does it.
- Office administrator: if you have or get an office administrator, make sure she or he is aligned with your team performance expectations, and learns and uses leadership skills to lead the team, day to day.

5. Annual Review of Your Strategic Plan

Things change: personal, personnel, economic, internal, and external. No one can predict the future. For these reasons and many more, review your strategic plan annually, from top to bottom. How many times has Post Raisin Bran been reinvented via "new and improved"? I don't know, but it seems it's in constant "new and improved" mode. I doubt if the raisin bran in the box is different, but it makes us consumers take a second look at it on the shelf. Your strategic plan, KPDs, and MPSR should be reviewed and updated annually. If not, they will become stale to your team members and to you. Think "new and improved"! Your plan will not necessarily need a makeover, although, for any number of reasons, a piece or two of your plan may need reevaluation to ensure it's doing what it's intended to do: drive performance to optimum production and keep your team engaged and consistently delivering exceptional experiences for your patients.

What if you hire an associate? What if you add two more rooms? What if you add another full-timer at the front desk or another full-time hygienist? Get the idea? Don't let your strategic plan become complacent.

You Achieved It! Make It Better!

I've discussed continuously improving your strategic plan and its supporting cast of KPDs and MPSR. I've discussed keeping a keen eye on the culprits that can negatively affect the results you and your team created, and the financial rewards you and you team can enjoy.

You and your team built it and everyone is enjoying the benefits. Stay focused. Prevent distractions. Lead your team to a long career of achievements!

The Bottom Line

You and your team built it and everyone is enjoying the benefits. Stay focused. Prevent distractions. Lead your team to a long career of achievements!

THE MOST SUCCESSFUL DENTAL PRACTICE OWNERS DO TWO THINGS:

1. They execute their up-to-date written strategic plan.
2. They stay focused on no more than five key production drivers.

The better the written strategic plan, the better the results. Admittedly, I have met a few dentists who do not have a written strategic plan, yet they have achieved exceptional successes. However, most dentists do not have a strategic plan and, therefore, do not have a well-thought-out road map to grow their practices and achieve their personal and professional goals.

Why this is so prevalent in the dental industry goes back to education, beginning with college majors, dental school, associations, and dental study groups. Their primary focus is, essentially, to enhance the excellence of dentistry, as it should be. While practice management speakers are often included in the curriculum of association meetings, access to deep and broad information on how to build a successful dental practice is not formally available unless through private-sector organizations. Therefore, the awareness, and the quantity and quality of knowledge needed to build an efficient and effective operational business is not a focus in the industry. Dental students, start-up dentists, and even mature dentists have to find their own way.

There are hundreds of practice management topics available to dentists through a variety of opportunities. Unfortunately, the subject of A to Z strategic planning from conception to results is, essentially, missing. Therefore, unless dentists access advisers, strategists, and/or consultants, they will not likely be exposed to critical pieces of the puzzle that are necessary to maximize the results and success of that business. And, by the way, this myopic view is true in many other industries. Having served several different industries, I have found that the main topics of conversation among business owners are about the products and services of their industry. Bank associations, for example, focus on banking products and services, not on the operational side of the business.

The Operational Focus

The drumbeat I hear often from dentists is that they need more new patients, more referrals, fewer no-shows and fewer cancellations. Just like every other business, you need to fill the schedule and keep the schedule full with qualified customers/patients. So, how are you going to do it effectively and efficiently? Go back to Chapter Three to fill the schedule. However, before you jump to a conclusion, evaluate why you are not filling the schedule now. If you don't fully and clearly answer the *why*, any action you take will not achieve the results you expect, because the core problem still will not have been resolved.

Know Why and Resolve the Why before You Act!

When the *why* is resolved, you are in a position to think about the most effective and efficient methods (that's planning) to accomplish your objective. But don't discount a second opinion, and maybe a third. Unless the evaluation fee is ridiculously high, get it done. It's an investment in finding the best solution as quickly as possible, because lost production is far more costly. How many months of losing out on $15,000+/- of production are worth waiting to find the best solutions for your practice? Trial and error is not a smart method of solving a problem or seeking the best solution, either. It's too cookie-cutter and not specific to the *why* of your practice. It's expensive, because topical solutions get topical results. And, as mentioned earlier, your team members are tired of being guinea pigs. Plus, it's very likely you will not be any closer to the real solution. I can hear it now: "But John, I prefer not to ask for advice." The truth is you already use advisers. You have supply and equipment advisers, a CPA, an insurance agent, and a financial adviser, to name a few. Talk to some of the professionals in the area of expertise you need. Don't buy their expertise unless the expertise is suited to your need. It's about getting all of the facts on the table and evaluating them. Once you do that, you can merge all of the information into a plan that is executable and has the highest opportunity of achieving the best results, the soonest, with the biggest return on investment for you and your practice.

Mindset

I was a few months from graduating from college. My father told me, "John, when you get into the world of making a living on your own, you are going to meet all kinds of people." That statement has played out many times since 1974. Whether it is a dentist, the owner of a plumbing company, or the owner of a start-up tech company, Dad was correct. I've certainly met all kinds of people.

- There are business owners who pretend to play the game of running a successful business but are afraid of building a team of advisors around them who can help grow their business as big and as fast as the owner desires.

- There are business owners who play not to lose. If the decision isn't 100 percent no-risk guaranteed, there is no decision. Opportunity after opportunity is lost and production suffers. Stagnation and mediocrity trickle down from the dentists to all of the team members.

- There are business owners who play to win...to finish. They do their due diligence, plan their strategy and tactics, get professional feedback, learn the potential negatives and the positives, and weigh both sides to make thoughtful and fact-based decisions. Sometimes it's *go* and sometimes it's *not yet*. When it's *go*, they are all in, decisive, persistent, and patient. Once in a while, the end result is a bust. Most often, the end result is a rousing success with celebration and excitement. That feeling of achievement creates more confidence, because they know that the process of evaluation and thoughtfulness on the front-end created the results on the back-end.

I have had the pleasure of serving dental practice owners who have an insatiable appetite to be the best they can be—personally and professionally—for the sake of their patients, team members, and families. Interestingly, few of these successful dentists keep score based on their personal income. It's more about their mindset, the personal satisfaction of seeing team members happy and enjoying being a part of something that is more than just a job. It's about being proud of building something, making something happen, finding innovative solutions, and looking back at the results. It's the proof that their well-thought-out plan guided them directly to their goals as they laughed at their mistakes along the way, which reminds me of another dad-ism. My first job out of college was a miserable one. I couldn't see how it had anything to do with my future. After I confided in my father, he said, "John, you will find many road blocks in life. You can go over the roadblock, around it, under it, or through it, but you can't stand there and stare at it. The roadblock is not going to disappear. You have to act!"

What are your roadblocks and what's your action?

There are plenty of dentists who clearly need to focus on optimizing production, collections, and profit right now. Every month matters. Every invoice and payroll cycle causes financial pain. All too often, the pain is clearly detectable on the faces of the dentist/owners. The urgency is deafening. Dentists have told me that they don't have time for this strategic planning thing. My response is, "You don't have time not to plan your way out of this!" It's the lack of planning, very likely, that caused the low production and lack of cash flow in the first place. A couple weeks of planning isn't going to make the problem worse. Very likely, it will solve the problem—and soon.

A few weeks ago, I delivered a written strategic plan to Dr. Rick. He had heard me speak at a study club meeting three years ago. He's a solo GP with two full-time hygienists producing $97,000 per month. While he was finishing with his last patient and I waited in his office to deliver and discuss his plan, I noticed his bookcase. One shelf contained five three-ring binders from his meetings with onsite consultants and participation in offsite practice-management immersion events. The second shelf had ten or more packages of DVDs and CDs from known consultants in the practice management category. The third shelf contained 15 or more books, all of which were authored by business thought-leaders in multiple industries. None of them are about the dental industry.

Rick had, apparently, been playing to win for a long time. His results clearly demonstrated his efforts to find real and sustainable solutions. About two-thirds of the way through the delivery of his strategic plan, he said, "John, I have been very fortunate over the years to have done quite well in my practice. I've tried to do the right things for my team and my patients. I've made a few colossal mistakes and plenty of other mistakes that I wish I could retract. Clearly, we have plenty of room to improve, so I invited you to my practice to help me plan my next ten years. Since I heard you at the study club presentation three years ago, I've been watching your successes and I've talked with some of my peers you have served. You have been vetted! Otherwise, we wouldn't be sitting here right now. You already know that making more money is way down on my list of priorities. You know I want to make sure that we are doing our best. You have met my team members and you have engaged in conversations with all of them. You know I have flown by the seat of my pants and you know that I am not bashful about asking for help. I have to tell you my team members were really nervous about my bringing you into our practice for the purposes of planning our future. But from the outset, you have engaged them in the planning conversations, and they feel their ideas matter, and on top of that, they even like you. You can offer an idea for discussion, knowing we need to use it, but you don't commit to it until they commit to it. That's brilliant! I'm very pleased with the manner in which you approach the planning process and only wish I had not waited three years to step back from the day-to-day work and truly plan for our future. This process is, without a doubt, the best thing I have ever done for my practice."

Rick, like so many of you, has the best of intentions. The problem, however, is getting from intentions to achieving your wishes, wants, and desires for your practice. Every dentist/owner has them. Few achieve them. What are yours? Will they continue to be wishes, wants, and desires, or will you *plan* to achieve them?

This book has been one of my big wishes, wants, and desires for three years. It allows me to share innovative, results-based strategies and tactics with many more dentists than I will ever have the pleasure of meeting. And that's a big check mark on my bucket list.

Now, you have the ball. I encourage you to run with it. Run strategically! Forget about making a few mistakes. We all do. Laugh them off. Press forward.

I encourage you to read this book one more time. Make notes in the margins. Highlight key points. Ask your team members to read the book. Get their feedback.

Last, but not least, take your first step. Actions beget rewards.

Make a note of the top five key things you will improve in your practice in the next 30 days.

1. _____

2. _____

3. _____

4. _____

5. _____

Because you read this book, you've earned a private conversation with me to discuss your top-five list. You have the ball! What are you going to do with it?

E-mail me at john@whydtp.com. We'll set a date and a time to talk!

Yesterday is history and it can't be improved! Today is yours to embrace. It's waiting for your leadership to make your hopes and dreams come true.